— SOBER —
BODY

A Guide to Health and Fitness in Sobriety

— SOBER —
BODY

A Guide to Health and Fitness in Sobriety

DIRK FOSTER

Sober Body: A Guide to Health and Fitness in Sobriety

ISBN (paperback):
eISBN:

CONTENTS

Website: www.thesoberjourney.com
Facebook: www.facebook.com/sobertravels/

Other Books by Dirk Foster:
**The Sober Journey: A Guide to Prayer
and Meditation in Recovery**

Get advice from a doctor first, then you can use this book later if you and your doctor feel it can help you.

Please be aware that the information being presented to you in the following pages is based on personal experience. I am not offering any medical advice. I am not a doctor nor do I claim to have any medical expertise, just my own personal experience as a recovering alcoholic who had many health problems in early recovery.

No Warranties: The authors and publishers don't guarantee or warrant the quality, accuracy, completeness, timeliness, appropriateness or suitability of the information in this book, or of any product or services referenced by this site. The information in this site is provided on an "as is" basis and the authors and publishers make no representations or warranties of any kind with respect to this information. This site may contain inaccuracies, typographical errors, or other errors.

Liability Disclaimer: The publishers, authors, and any other parties involved in the creation, production, provision of information, or delivery of this book and related sites specifically disclaim any responsibility, and shall not be liable for any damages, claims, injuries, losses, liabilities, costs or obligations including any direct, indirect, special, incidental, or consequential damages (collectively known as "Damages") whatsoever and howsoever caused, arising out of, or in connection with, the use or misuse of the site and the information contained within it, whether such Damages arise in contract, tort, negligence, equity, statute law, or by way of any other legal theory.

This book is dedicated to Eric Steglich; A good man, beautiful and bright, who battled his addictions the best he could, but lost the war. May you rest in peace, dear friend.

PART ONE

SICK AND TIRED OF BEING SICK AND TIRED

*"The journey of a thousand miles
begins with a single step."*
~ Tao Te Ching

*"Fat, drunk and stupid is no way
to go through life, son."*
~ Dean Wormer, Animal House

A DAY IN THE LIFE

Every day it's the same thing. I wake up around noon. The sunlight pierces my eyes like a knife. I'm disoriented, confused, not sure where I am or how I got here. Am I home? Am I in a motel room? Am I in a bed? Am I in an alley? *Where the hell am I, and how did I get here?*

As the brain fog slowly begins to clear, I'm able to piece together a few simple thoughts; vague images of the night before including the holy trinity of drinking, cocaine and cigarettes. How did I get into bed? I don't remember. Who was I with? What did I do that I'll regret later? Were the police involved? Did I hurt anybody?

I try to stir my body, but it feels like I've been hit by a train. Every bone and muscle hurts. My head is *pounding, pounding, pounding.* Bitter bile rises from my stomach to meet my throat. Nausea comes in waves. The taste in my mouth is foul, like I've been nibbling on dog shit appetizers. The smell of my own breath meets my nostrils making me wretch.

I notice the familiar trembling, the horrible tremors that I dread each morning. My body is rattling, shaking from the inside. Every organ is shivering, not from cold but from poisoning, rejecting what I've forced upon them, fighting for survival.

I lie there, shaking, slightly confused, frightened. How did I get here again? Every day it's the same damn thing!

I roll over and try to stand. My body feels battered and weak. It takes all my effort to stand and stumble to the bathroom.

I look at my face in the mirror, bloated and puffy; watery eyes; oily hair; yellowing teeth; dry skin. I barely recognize myself anymore. I'm 42 years old but I could easily pass for 62. I look worn out, exhausted, spent. I've put on so much weight I can't see my feet over my stomach. The idea of living a long life never crosses my mind anymore. I know it's just a matter of time before my body gives up on me; I'm rotting from the inside.

I fall to my knees and purge the contents of my stomach into the toilet, a deluge of liquid that smells like vodka and beer.

Another day has begun.

***

Greasy food! That's what I need! That's what is going to help me get through this horrendous hangover.

Now my goal becomes very simple; get a huge cheeseburger, a large order of french fries and a chocolate milk shake. That's what will save me!

After I guzzle down a pot of coffee and smoke several cigarettes I head outside into the miserable daylight and head to McDonald's. Even though it's only a few blocks away, I drive. Why bother walking?

I return home with my bag of greasy grub and drop like a stone onto the couch. I eat, watch crappy TV shows, and smoke half a pack of cigarettes. I have no fresh water in my apartment so I drink tap water that tastes like dirty shoes.

Throughout the day I tell myself that I won't drink tonight no matter what. Enough is enough. I need to slow down. I'm going to take a night off. I'll get a good night's sleep and in the morning I'll rise early, refreshed, and take a long walk. Maybe I'll even jog a few blocks just to work up a good sweat. I'm going to start eating better tomorrow. I'll load up the refrigerator with fresh fruits and vegetables, lean protein and a case of spring water. That's what I need, I tell myself; sleep, exercise, and healthy food.

My new resolution to get healthy cheers me up. I feel less hungover, the tremors have subsided. The pounding in my head is less severe. I manage to slip off into a semi-restful nap, haunted by strange dreams.

When I wake up from my nap I feel better. I light a cigarette and head to the kitchen for some tap water. As I drink the foul tasting water I notice the half-empty liter of Smirnoff vodka on top of the refrigerator. I stare at it, transfixed, like a moth contemplating a flame. It seems to be staring back at me, waiting.

Tomorrow is a new day. I'm going to start fresh and healthy, I tell myself. I'm going eat right, exercise and stop drinking so much.

It's four o'clock in the afternoon. I'm feeling optimistic and excited about the new life I'm going to start tomorrow. Maybe I'll have just one shot to celebrate my new life that starts tomorrow. No big deal. Tomorrow's going to be awesome! I can't wait for tomorrow!

I grab the vodka bottle. This is going to be the last time. I pour a small shot, not a full one. No reason to get carried away.

I quickly toss it back; feel the familiar burn down my throat and the soothing warmth through my body. Ease and comfort arises.

Tomorrow is going to be great! I can't wait for tomorrow. I'm going to start a whole new health regimen.

I pour another shot, a full one this time. I drink it fast.

The burn... the ease... the comfort.

I quickly pour a third shot, chasing after the sensation running through my body. It feels too good. Why stop now?

It begins again, the same today as every day. I pour another shot.

SICK AND TIRED

The last few years of my life as an active alcoholic were spent in a repetitive cycle of days like the one I just described. I had reached a point where I merely existed from one day to the next in a haze of alcohol abuse, minimal sleep, horrible diet, and no exercise (unless you consider lifting a vodka bottle to be exercise). I spent most of my time in my dark apartment, curtains closed, with very little interaction with normal people. It was a very lonely and unhealthy life, and I needed help to climb out of the hole I had dug.

Through the grace of God and the fellowship of a 12-Step program, I was able to break the cycle of addiction that I had been drowning in for more than three decades, finally getting sober at age 43. Getting and staying sober has been the most difficult and challenging experience of my entire life, and I am forever grateful that I asked for the help I so desperately needed. I've been sober now for 12 years and can't imagine ever going back to the life I once lived.

Gone are the days of suffering, loneliness and poor health. But how did I get here? How did I climb out of the dark hole and build a healthy, productive life for myself?

First, *I had become sick and tired of being sick and tired.* Before getting sober, I was miserable all the time, depressed, and constantly sick. Nothing made me feel better; not even the alcohol I consumed every day could lift me out of my misery. But, as any alcoholic will attest, I kept drinking, hoping that it would bring me the peace and comfort I so desperately craved. But at some point even the alcohol stopped working. Nothing made me feel better anymore.

During the final stretch of my addiction, I was in very bad shape physically (mentally and spiritually, as well). My body was starting to give up on me. My doctor informed me that I had fatty liver, dangerously high blood pressure, and elevated cholesterol levels. My skin, hair and teeth were showing signs of early decay. I was grossly overweight and could barely walk up a short flight of stairs without wheezing. I had been smoking up to two packs of cigarettes per day for years, so my lungs were sore and straining. My digestion was horrible, and I suffered from constant stomach pain and diarrhea (*too much detail?*). My sleeping patterns were erratic, and I always felt tired and fatigued. Over the last few years, I went to the hospital several times with chest pains (fortunately, these pains were from anxiety attacks and not actual heart attacks).

In addition to the vast quantities of alcohol and cigarettes I consumed every day, and the drugs I often took,

I lived on a steady diet of junk food. My typical meals were burgers, fries and milk shakes. When I was low on money, which was often, I would skip eating all together in order to buy my booze and cigarettes for the night.

I was living an unhealthy and desperate lifestyle, like a rat trapped in a cage of addiction.

Once I had a couple months of sobriety under my belt (*with my belly still hanging* way *over my belt*), I took a cold, hard look at my physical condition and was appalled. I knew I had to do something about repairing my body, as well as my mind and spirit. I knew I was still in a very dangerous and precarious situation because of all the abuse I had inflicted upon my body over the years. I needed further healing beyond just not drinking.

It was then I began to explore what had happened to me as a result of my addiction and what I could do to reverse the damage.

I knew that it wasn't going to be an easy path. I had beaten up my body for so long, and I wasn't even sure if I could ever fully recover my health. But I was determined to learn and try. I wanted to live. And I wanted to live a healthy, vibrant, productive life free from alcohol and drugs, and filled with smart choices (including what I ate and how I could repair my body).

I want to share with you what I learned, what I did, and how positive and miraculous the results have been for me and many other people who have taken the same journey; a journey of rejuvenation, joy and hope in recovery.

And there is hope for you, too.

Don't be discouraged by anything you read in the following pages. I'm going to present to you an overview of what alcohol and drugs do to our bodies and what we can do to overcome the damage we have inflicted on ourselves. I will present an easy-to-follow guide that will show you how simple it can be to rebuild your health from the inside out so that you can, hopefully, get back the energy, strength and longevity that you deserve. In terms of my own recovery, here's a partial list of results:

- ☑ Significant weight loss (40 pounds)
- ☑ Eliminated hypertension
- ☑ Eliminated high cholesterol
- ☑ Eliminated stomach pain
- ☑ Eliminated fatty liver
- ☑ Improved hair and skin
- ☑ Improved sleep patterns
- ☑ Improved muscle tone
- ☑ Improved cardio endurance
- ☑ Improved mood and temper
- ☑ Improved clarity and memory
- ☑ Improved state of mind (happier and more optimistic)

Changing your health habits can and will significantly and positively affect your body, mind and spirit. It's never too late to start anew, no matter how old you are. You have been given just one body which should be respected and treated with care. Love your body as a temple, a unique form given to you by God (or Mother Nature, if you prefer). Sobriety is about new beginnings and new adventures. The journey of a thousand miles begins with a single step. So let's take the first step together on your new journey of hope, health and recovery.

THE DAMAGE DONE

Let's get right to the point: every time you pour alcohol down your throat, snort cocaine, shoot heroin, or smoke crack or meth, you're poisoning your body. This probably isn't news to you, but it's something most addicts CHOOSE to ignore in pursuit of their next fix.

Alcohol is one of the worst things you can put into your body. It wreaks havoc on your entire system. There's not a single thing in alcohol that your body needs or wants. Cocaine and heroin, as well as other street drugs, serve no purpose other than to temporarily change how you feel. Otherwise, they're pointless.

But with addicts, sometimes having no point *is the point*. When we're drinking or using, we're seeking relief and oblivion, not health and improvement. We want to numb ourselves to the point where we don't care what the point is, and that's the whole point.

Alcohol and drug abuse impacts every part of your body, and not in a good way. They can, and do, lead to abnormal heart rate; destruction of internal organs (especially the liver and kidneys); diminished brain function; decaying bones; rotting teeth; hair loss and dry skin; and damaged lungs. These are just a few of the physical manifestations associated with long term substance abuse. Long term addiction has also been proven to cause depression, sleep loss and anxiety as well as dementia and certain forms of cancer.

Even though most of us know how destructive substance abuse is for the human body, we consume them anyway, over and over, sometimes until we lose everything we love. The most unfortunate among us often lose their lives.

If apples were proven to be poisonous to your bodies, would you stay up all night eating one apple after another? If almonds could kill you, would you chop them into dust and snort them or shoot them into your veins? The fact is you wouldn't. But apples and almonds don't make you feel high so why bother, right?

But we know without doubt that every time we drink, snort, inhale or shoot our substance of choice, we're slowly poisoning ourselves drop by drop, grain by grain.

And it's not just the long term effects that should be a glaring warning. Even the short term effects are brutal on your body. Think about how bad the hangovers are or how often you threw up, passed out, crashed your car, or ended up in the hospital. All of these occurrences are the direct and immediate result of putting poison into your body in order to briefly alter how you think and feel.

The definition of insanity is repeating the same thing over and over but expecting a different result. It's the same thing with the poison we put into our bodies as addicts. Day in and day out, we consume the poison but then wonder why we always feel like shit and can't get anything done. Or why we keep landing in the hospital. Or why our friends and family start avoiding us. Or why our friends keep dying from their addictions.

Our insanity becomes a way of life and will kill us unless we're willing to take the proper steps to reverse the damage.

---

*Health Tip: One of the most powerful gifts we have as human beings is our ability to forgive. The first gift you can give to yourself in your recovery is forgiveness. Let's face it, we all screwed things up with our drinking and using. But if we want to move forward and regain our health, we first need to forgive ourselves. It probably won't happen all at once, but take the first step forward by forgiving yourself.

EARLY RECOVERY

et's be honest; early recovery can be brutal. This is just a fact and if you haven't discovered it already, then you probably will if you're new to sobriety or trying to get sober.

I could try to convince you that the early stage of recovery is all about rainbows, butterflies and unicorns and that you're going to feel instantly amazing every single day, as if new sobriety is one giant, continuous orgasm. But that would be a lie and my intention is to be as straightforward and honest as I can. Often, early sobriety is about being pounded day and night by a storm of painful feelings and emotions. This is just the reality of what we have to face in order to get clean and stay clean.

At first, new sobriety can be a wonderful experience in many ways. Just the clarity of mind that occurs from not drinking or using can feel like a miracle. But usually after a few days or weeks, we start to experience those damn things called "feelings" which can overwhelm us. Some of the feelings are great. Some of the feelings truly suck. Sometimes they're pleasant. Sometimes they're painful. But the feelings start to come fast and furious and can occasionally scare people who are new to recovery.

When you think about it, we've spent years (in most cases) trying to hide from, or suppress, our feelings with booze and drugs. For whatever reason, most addicts hate feeling much of anything other than feeling high and euphoric. For whatever reason, we try to avoid any discomfort in our lives; at some point we discovered that alcohol and dope are the easiest and fastest ways to escape a wide range of feelings and emotions. We prefer numbness to just about everything else. But once you take away those numbing agents, we start to experience a flood of mental, emotional and even physical feelings that we haven't felt in years, sometimes decades.

I remember how incredibly uncomfortable I felt in the world when I first got sober. I didn't know how to act, talk, react, engage or socialize in any way, shape or form. In many ways, I had to restart my entire life. I had to be reborn into the world of adult socialization and conversation. It was an incredibly awkward time for me, coupled with the fact that I'm naturally shy and struggle with social anxiety. Thankfully, I was living in Los Angeles at the time and had many 12-Step meetings to go to every day of the week. Slowly I began surrounding myself with recovering addicts, which gave me an opportunity to relearn how to communicate and interact with other adults without having to rely on cocktails to get me through social situations.

But even worse than the social anxiety was the physical pain and discomfort I experienced in early recovery. My body was trashed from all the substance abuse I had forced upon it for many years. I had lived on a steady diet of alcohol, drugs and cigarettes for decades, and my body was desperate to repair itself.

In those early days I could hardly sleep at all and would often break out in a cold sweat as my body worked to squeeze out all the toxins that had pooled in every pore of my body. I would sweat so much at night that I had to keep buying new pillowcases to replace the ones that were stained permanently yellow (*sexy, I know*). My skin was blotchy and dry, which made me feel more self-conscious than normal (which is saying a lot). I often felt my heart racing so fast it felt like it might explode. I suffered with extreme levels of anxiety and paranoia and became deeply depressed. I frequently had bad headaches and worst of all; my stomach was in constant agony. I had horrible pain and discomfort in my belly morning, noon and night. There were times that it became almost unbearable. Of course, being a hypochondriac at the time, I convinced myself that I had stomach cancer and that I would die soon (*a quick shout-out to my first sponsor, Paul C, for patiently putting up with all my complaining, whining and panic attacks in those early days. You're an angel, brother.*).

Yet somehow I managed to stay sober one day at a time, for which I am forever grateful.

After a few months, I began to feel a little better but I still never felt great. So about six months into my recovery I made the decision to change the way I felt by learning everything I could about what I had done to my health and how I could try to repair some of the lingering damage that still plagued me.

....

Health Tip: *One of the best ways to improve your health is by getting at least eight hours of sleep every night. This might be difficult at first, so take a few naps throughout the day. Even just a 15 minute "power nap" can do wonders for your mental and physical strength.*

STOMACH DAMAGE

I want to start by discussing alcohol's effect on the stomach because, as I mentioned earlier, stomach pain was one of the worst parts of my early sobriety. The pain and discomfort was unbearable at times. There were times when the pain was so bad I couldn't leave the house. I would just lay on the couch all day hugging a heated blanket, moaning and praying for the agony to end.

Part of the problem I faced was psychosomatic, no doubt about it. I was learning to live without alcohol, so I was experiencing intense anxiety and fear which certainly added to my stomach problems. This level of stress is guaranteed to cause anyone physical issues like stomach pain, headaches and depression. The psychological strain I was under certainly added to the physical discomfort I was suffering through.

I also discovered through research that large quantities of alcohol consumed over many years will cause a tremendous amount of damage to the stomach lining. Alcohol acts like a corrosive acid on your stomach lining and internal organs. Over time, this acidic barrage can cause gastritis, ulcers, reflux (heartburn) and diminishes nutrient absorption. A brief explanation of each follows:

- ☑ **Gastritis**—Inflammation of the stomach lining which can cause long term pain, nausea, vomiting and irritable bowel syndrome. If left untreated for long enough, gastritis can be fatal.
- ☑ **Ulcers**—Painful sores in the stomach due to excessive acid and deterioration of the stomach lining.
- ☑ **Reflux**—Alcohol can, and very often does, cause gastric fluids in the stomach to rise up to the esophagus. Reflux causes a burning sensation in the throat and can cause nausea and vomiting. Esophageal cancer is one of the most common forms of cancer among alcoholics.
- ☑ **Nutrition**—Long term alcohol abuse often results in diminished appetite, which causes stress to the stomach lining and can result in further deterioration of the stomach wall.

So what's the bottom line? If you drank as much as I did for as long as I did, your stomach might be a complete mess when you first get sober. If you have experienced any level of pain, discomfort or grumbling in your belly in early recovery, most likely you have done some damage to the lining of your stomach.

The good news is that with time and some simple nutritional changes you can reverse the damage.

But you have to be patient. The very fact that you're no longer pouring liquid acid (alcohol) into your body is a great first step. But you also will need to develop some wise eating habits which I will discuss later. For now, if you're having stomach pain and discomfort in early recovery, just know that it's common and even normal and won't last forever (*if the pain is severe or you experience bleeding, please consult a physician*).

Over time, with a few simple dietary changes coupled with more sleep and a body that no longer consumes alcohol, your stomach pain will diminish and hopefully disappear.

....

*Health Tip: If you need temporary relief from stomach pain, a glass of milk can quickly coat your stomach and bring some relief. Also, over-the-counter products like Pepto Bismol can help diminish stomach discomfort. These are short term solutions, but they can help.

LIVER DAMAGE

Most people are aware that the liver takes the biggest beating when it comes to excessive alcohol consumption. Booze wreaks havoc on our livers. Long-term heroin and cocaine abuse also inflict major damage on the liver as well.

The main function of your liver is to filter and detoxify the blood that enters your digestive tract before it passes through the rest of your body. In other words, it cleanses the blood before allowing it to enter other areas of your body. It's amazing, if you think about it. We have a built-in system for cleaning and distributing what we put into our bodies to ensure we are reaping the maximum benefits while discarding anything that might harm us (toxins).

The problem occurs when we bombard the liver with too much alcohol which it is unable to process in a normal fashion. Eventually, chronic alcohol abuse begins to damage the liver cells which can result in scarring of the liver walls, which in turn can progress to *fatty liver, alcoholic hepatitis, cirrhosis,* and sometimes *liver cancer.*

The bottom line, alcohol is brutal to your liver. Heavy drinkers face a very high risk of developing numerous forms of liver disease especially after many years of hard and persistent boozing (*raise your hand if this sounds like you*). This is especially true for those of us who get sober in middle age. The longer we wait to get sober, the more susceptible we become to the ravages of alcohol abuse on our livers and other internal organs.

Some common symptoms of liver damage include:

- ☑ Yellowish skin and eyes ("jaundice")
- ☑ Abdominal pain and swelling
- ☑ Swelling in legs and ankles
- ☑ Dark urine
- ☑ Nausea or vomiting
- ☑ Itchy skin
- ☑ Discolored stool
- ☑ Tendency to bruise easily
- ☑ Chronic fatigue
- ☑ Fever and sweating
- ☑ Frequent disorientation
- ☑ Physical weakness
- ☑ Loss of appetite

If you've noticed any of these symptoms, you need to consider that you might have inflicted some damage to your liver. But all is not lost. Assuming you've begun your sober journey and are willing to take a few

simple steps, there is a pathway back to better health
and includes repairing the damage to your liver.

....

***Health Tip**: *Green tea is known to help cleanse and revitalize the
liver. Try drinking a few cups of whole leaf green tea several times
each day. Add a little honey for sweetener.*

BRAIN DAMAGE

I f you've successfully read this far into this book and were able to comprehend most of what I've written, then chances are your brain is probably still working pretty well. Congratulations!

Nevertheless, abusing drugs and alcohol is known to cause brain damage, even with mild to moderate usage. And it's important to have a basic understanding of what you may have done to your brain while you were using.

In a nutshell, alcohol and drug abuse effect the brain in the following ways:

- ☑ Blocking nutrients that a healthy brain needs to function
- ☑ Destruction of brain cells and neurotransmitter receptors
- ☑ Altering brain chemical composition and construction
- ☑ Depriving proper flow of oxygen to brain tissues

This is just a simple overview of the damage we can do to our brain every time we drink to excess, shoot up, snort a line or pop a pill. Extensive and long term substance abuse can and does result in destruction of brain cells, and our ability to think clearly and intelligently. Ultimately it can result in making really bad decisions (like drinking *more* and using *more*); memory loss; visual disorientation; hallucinations; loss of physical coordination; dementia; sickness and death. One of the more well-known results of excessive alcohol abuse is "wet brain," a chronic brain disorder which may result in permanent damage.

The more we abuse alcohol and drugs, the more likely we are to damage our brains which results in our inability to make normal decisions. We become trapped in an endless loop of drinking, using, and bad decisions due to the fact that we are altering the chemical structure of our brain so that our thought process becomes jumbled and, quite simply, STUPID.

We literally drink ourselves stupid!

In order to reverse the process and repair the damage, we need to feed every part of our body with proper nutrients that will restore our damaged brain cells, as well as getting a proper amount of sleep and establishing an exercise routine that we enjoy. With time and patience, hopefully we'll start making more smart choices and fewer stupid ones as our brains rejuvenate and we regain our ability to think clearly, make positive decisions, and improve our memory.

Now if only I could remember where I parked my car…

....

*****Health Tip**: *Certain types of fish are known to improve brain function. Try eating fish several times per week that are high in omega-3 fatty acids and vitamin D, such as salmon, mackerel and sardines. Oysters are also healthy brain food.*

MUSCLE DAMAGE

The sad truth is that most alcoholics and addicts spend more time at the bar than the gym. We prefer twelve ounce curls to twelve pound curls, and it shows in our physical appearance by the time most of us get sober. Yes, there is the rare exception of an addict who runs marathons or is a champion athlete or goes to the gym every day. But those people are the exception, certainly not the rule.

Most of us, when we finally manage to get sober, are in poor physical shape. We wheeze walking up stairs. We tire easily. We can barely lift anything heavier than a cigarette. Our bodies, in most cases, are used and abused, and it shows in our posture, our weight and in our poor muscle development.

Let's face it, most of us start our sobriety like newborn babies; weak, pudgy, helpless and crying.

Muscle atrophy is one of the most common physical attributes shared by addicts who are newly sober. While there isn't necessarily a direct link between alcohol (or drug) abuse and muscle atrophy, there is certainly a direct link associated with the sedentary lives most of us lead as practicing addicts. We spend the majority of our waking hours in non-physical pursuits—drinking at the bar, drinking at home, drinking in front of the television, calling the dealer, etc.

By the time we finally get sober, we've spent so many years sitting on our asses drinking and using that we're about as physically strong and healthy as a worm (or more accurately, a tequila worm).

Muscle atrophy is simply when muscle wastes away from lack of use. Once our muscles begin to disintegrate, we become less and less interested in physical activity (exercise in particular) due to the extra amount of effort and exertion it now takes to accomplish. Eventually we just stop trying as we continue to numb our brains in our quest for oblivion.

I clearly remember how difficult it was for me to perform the most basic physical tasks when I first got sober. Cleaning my apartment left me exhausted. Walking a few blocks seemed like a monumental task. Lifting a few weights at the gym seemed like an impossible (and miserable) task which I wanted to avoid at all costs.

But it's imperative that we begin to rebuild our muscle structure. And the sooner we get started, the better we'll feel and the more opportunities we'll have to enjoy a wider variety of activities—things like hiking, walking, biking, fishing and yoga to name just a few.

Muscle strength is one of the most important aspects of a healthy, strong body. Therefore, we need to do whatever we can to rebuild and repair the muscle atrophy that has reduced us to weak baby worms.

....

***Health Tip**: *Start walking! We'll explore this topic further in other sections of this book. But for now, make a point to take a short walk (or two) each day. Even just fifteen minutes of walking will help build your leg muscles and increase your endurance. Get out of the house and take a walk!*

TOOTH AND GUM DAMAGE

'm going to let you in on a little secret. And please don't take offense. Just accept the fact I'm going to present and deal with it. Okay, here it goes...

If you've been abusing alcohol, cigarettes, hard drugs or any combination of these three things over the last few years (or worse, 10 or 20 years), your teeth and gums are suffering and your breath stinks. Does that sound mean? Sorry, it's just a fact.

Anyone who has been an active addict for any length of time has done damage to their teeth and gums. Additionally your digestive systems is unhealthy (see Chapter 6 "Stomach Damage") which means you're producing too much bile and acid which adds to the inevitable stench coming out of your mouth.

Alcohol has a high sugar content which causes damage to your gums, teeth and tongue. Likewise, alcohol causes dehydration and dry mouth, which results in decay and infection. Cocaine (especially when smoked) has a terrible impact on your teeth, rotting them quickly. I once knew a coke addict whose teeth literally began dropping out of his mouth when he brushed his teeth. He didn't experience any pain when they dropped out. They just fell effortless into the bathroom sink with a sad clink on the porcelain. Not the nicest way to start your morning.

There are volumes of information on the harm that cigarettes do to your teeth and gums. If you're a smoker, cigarettes have a huge impact on the health of your mouth as well as every other part of your body. Any non-smoker will tell you that kissing a smoker is as pleasant as licking a dirty ashtray.

So the bottom line is this: most likely your mouth has suffered as much as the rest of your body from your addiction.

One of the first things you need to do (if you can afford it) is visit a dentist to get an assessment of the damage done and what you need to do about it. Additionally, your diet will have a huge impact on the health of your teeth, gums and tongue. As you begin to improve your diet, over time you will also begin to experience an improvement in your oral hygiene.

....

*Health Tip: *Stay hydrated. In addition to brushing and flossing your teeth several times per day, water is very effective in diminishing bad breath and cleansing your mouth. Keep a bottle of water with you at all times and drink it all day, every day.*

SKIN AND HAIR DAMAGE

When I first got sober I was shocked by the poor condition of my skin and hair. My skin was red, blotchy and dry, especially on my face and hands. My hair, which had always been thick and blonde (*I've always been vain about my hair, I admit it*), was now thin, dry and darker than normal. When I came out of the stupor of my addiction I barely recognized myself. I clearly remember feeling like Rip Van Winkle, the fairytale character who slept for 20 years, then woke up to find everything about himself and the world has changed.

It was very depressing. I had done serious damages to myself and it showed.

Similar to the effects alcohol has on the health of your teeth and gums, it also dehydrates your skin and hair. The result of long term drinking can result in dry and brittle hair follicles as well as dry, flaking skin. It also diminishes the proper circulation of nutrients through your body.

Every time you drink or use, you're depriving your body of important nutrients. Alcohol and drugs block vitamins, proteins, minerals, carbohydrates and healthy fats from circulating properly throughout your system, all of which are essential to the health of your skin and hair. Your hair and skin require as much healthy nourishment as the rest of your body. No part of your body is immune from the damage of long term alcohol (or drug) abuse, and it does have a negative effect on your appearance.

Once you've stopped dumping alcohol into your system (and any other intoxicants) your skin and hair can begin to rejuvenate through proper hydration and nutrition. You'll be amazed at how quickly your body repairs itself with just a few simple adjustments to your diet.

....

*Health Tip: *Use hydrating shampoo on your hair and moisturizer on your skin. And hydrate with water as I mentioned before. Drink water morning, noon and night.*

WEIGHT GAIN AND HYPERTENSION

Alcohol and drug abuse, and the lifestyle that normally accompanies long term addiction, often leads to weight gain and high blood pressure (hypertension). It would be difficult to find a person who is new to recovery that doesn't suffer from an elevated heart rate and an increased level of fat around their body.

Alcohol in particular will increase your body mass due its high sugar content. Drinking vast amounts of booze over an extended period of time is like living on a steady diet of ice cream, candy bars and soda. Eventually it's going to catch up with you, resulting in substantial weight gain.

Likewise, alcohol increases the amount of fats in your bloodstream resulting in damage to your arteries which can lead to hypertension if left untreated. These hardened arties also increase the chance of blood clots which can, and often do, cause heart attacks and strokes in addicts. Not a pretty picture, but something we need to be very aware if we want to live long, healthy, sober lives.

Prior to getting sober my doctor informed me that I was suffering from fatty liver and pre-hypertension. At the time I weighed 200 pounds. For a man who is 5' 8", my healthy weight should be closer to 155 pounds. When I finally got clean, I was appalled at how heavy I was. I couldn't see my own feet when I looked down. Walking up a flight of stairs felt like climbing Mount Everest. I wheezed every time I crossed the living room. Each time I checked my blood pressure at the local pharmacy it registered so high I thought my heart was about to explode in my chest. I became seriously paranoid I was going to have a heart attack at any minute.

It took time to reduce the weight, I won't lie. I struggled with the pounds over the first year of my sobriety. But I was determined to shed the extra weight and began to focus on diet and exercise as a way to reach my goal. I recommend you do the same thing. With some time and effort, you can reduce your weight and blood pressure, and hopefully, get your heart rate back to normal.

....

Health Tip: Eating salty foods can lead to high blood pressure. Try to reduce the amount of salt in your diet. One of the fastest ways to do this is by avoiding fast food restaurants. Also, try to use less salt when cooking and eating.

SLEEP DISORDER

Have you ever seen those never-ending My-Pillow® television commercials? They come on at night... EVERY NIGHT! If you're an addict, most likely you've been up past the midnight hour many times and have seen these mildly annoying, but oddly likeable, infomercials. But what's most interesting is the man behind the company. Mike Lindell, the inventor of the MyPillow®, is a recovering addict, who once stayed up for two weeks straight smoking crack.

Thankfully, he's been sober for years. The first time I heard his story of addiction I felt sick, mostly because I could relate to his story so well. I never stayed up for two weeks straight (I doubt I would have survived that long of a bender), but there were many times when I was up for two or three days without sleep. Those are some of the most painful and awful memories I have from my addiction years, and I pray I never return to those times.

Anyone who has ever led a lifestyle of addiction filled with alcohol, cocaine or speed will have plenty of stomach churning stories about multi-day benders; epic tales of repeating sunrises that leave an indelible stain upon our memories. Even as I sit here writing this paragraph, I'm haunted by the memories I still have of those long ago days of depravity and sorrow as I chased the buzz through multiple nights without stopping.

If you have been a practicing addict for any length of time you are sleep deprived, I promise you that. Our bodies need sleep to survive and function properly. The average adult requires seven to eight hours of sound sleep every day. If we suffer from a lack of sound sleep, the damage to our bodies, and our ability to think clearly is profound. When we're drinking and using on a regular basis, we don't sleep so much as we *pass out*. Any sleep we get is usually restless and disturbing. And then we wake up with those damn hangovers, our bodies battling against the poison we've been ingesting.

One of the biggest challenges we face in early recovery is getting the correct amount of sleep each night. Even though we're no longer drinking and using, we're now struggling with a host of anxieties, fears and phobias that we spent years trying to suppress with booze and drugs. Ironic, isn't it? So now we're clean and sober, but we still don't sleep enough because we're dealing with all those damn feelings, anxieties and memories that we've been trying to run from our entire lives.

Over time, as your sobriety continues and you improve your health through diet and exercise, you will begin to sleep better. Besides diet and exercise, meditation will also bring great benefits and rest into your life. It might take time, and there will be restless nights when sadness, sorrow and regret wage war in your head. However, you need to hold fast and never give up. Sleep will come eventually as you move further and deeper into your sober journey.

....

Health Tip: *There are many plant-based sleep aids which you can buy at any natural food store. This might help you get more sleep at night. Also, I mentioned this earlier but it bears repeating; take a short nap every day if you can. A 15-30 minute nap will do wonders for your mind, body and spirit.*

A FEW WORDS ON BUTTS

Let's talk for a moment about butts. It seems that every addict loves butts. I was a butt addict myself. I was a real butt man. I loved butts. I had butts every day. Morning, noon and night I enjoyed butts. However, I gave up butts long ago, and I'm much happier and healthier now that I no longer have butts in my life.

Get your mind out of the gutter. I'm talking about cigarette butts, you weirdo.

Cigarettes seem to dangle from the lips of just about every addict who is new to recovery. If you're a 12-Stepper like me, you'll know what it's like to pass through the thick cloud of cigarette smoke floating outside of every meeting. Sometimes there's so much smoke near the front door of a 12-Step meeting that it looks like smog has settled around the building.

I'm not going to spend much time talking about the harm cigarettes cause to the human body. They are, quite simply, the absolute worst thing you can inflict upon yourself. They're terrible and most likely will lead you toward a very brutal, long death from cancer, emphysema, COPD, stroke or heart disease.

I encourage you to either quit or slow down on the number of cigarettes you smoke each day, with the goal of quitting entirely.

It's a very difficult thing to give up cigarettes, especially when you're new to sobriety and dealing with so many other things. But if you think about it, you're probably going through so much discomfort and anxiety anyway; why not just give up the smokes while you're at it. You're going to have to give them up eventually, why not just get it over with now?

If you can't give them up completely right now, try to cut your intake in half over a couple weeks. If you smoke two cigarettes every hour, cut back to just one. Or set aside a half pack in the morning and commit to only smoking those that day and no more. Come up with your own system, but the bottom line is you need to stop smoking the butts as soon as you can. Otherwise they'll catch up to you one way or another, and it won't be pretty, believe me.

So get off your butt and get off the butts.

....

Health Tip: *If you have a friend who also wants to quit smoking, form a support team, create a plan, set a goal and encourage each other along the journey until you both stop.*

INTO ACTION

The time to start is now! There is no reason to delay another hour or another day. Recovering your health is possible if you're just willing to make a few minor adjustments to your daily routine.

In the following pages, we will discuss a variety of topics that are focused on nutrition, exercise and health. Then we will go over mental and spiritual issues that are equally important to your long-term development and health. This book is designed so that you can jump from one section to another whenever you wish, depending on what you want to focus on. I suggest that the first time you read it, go from start to finish to get a clear picture of what it contains. Then later you can concentrate on specific areas of your health journey that are most important to you at that moment.

Here's the bottom line, and the point of this book: you've managed to get sober, or you're at least trying to get sober. Maybe you've been sober for one day, one year, or ten years. But you've made the honorable and smart decision to change and improve your life.

Getting clean and sober is the first and most important part of the journey you're on. But getting sober and being healthy are two different things.

I want you to be sober AND healthy. We do a lot of damage to our body, mind and spirit when we're out there drinking and using. Now it's your turn to reverse some of that damage and rebuild your body to where it wants to be, should be, and deserves to be.

You deserve the best that life has to offer. And your best begins right here, right now. The journey to full recovery is closer than you think. If you're just willing to take a few simple steps to get there, you'll discover the life you've always wanted.

Let's get started.

PART TWO

YOU ARE WHAT YOU EAT

*"Our bodies are our gardens; our
wills are our gardeners."*
~ William Shakespeare

FOOD IS FUEL

As the saying goes, *you are what you eat*. What you put into your body everyday has an immediate impact on every aspect of your physical and mental health.

I lived on a steady diet of booze, cigarettes and fast food for so long that I suffered serious health issues as a result of my lifestyle. For me, early sobriety was about much more than just learning how to live without alcohol every day. I also needed to learn, or relearn, how to fuel my body with the right food that would help me rebuild and recharge it. I had to replace the toxins I was dumping into my body with the natural fuel of healthy food.

Good food is a gift. Food is one of the great pleasures of life given to us by God. If you can learn how to appreciate food not only for how it tastes but also how it sustains you, you will be more likely to make wise choices every time you eat. Your body is a natural engine that requires a constant input of fuel in order to run properly over a long period of time (many, many years, I hope). So it's imperative that you fill your body-engine with only the best fuel possible. Respect your body and your body will show you respect. It's as simple as that.

This isn't to say you can't indulge in sweets and even junk food occasionally. We're not talking about complete denial of food that is fun and even fattening. I personally love ice cream and sweets. My wife and I love to have pancakes occasionally for breakfast. And we sometimes eat french fries and turkey burgers.

I've spent a lot of time in 12-Step meetings over the years. Quite often there is a table filled with cookies, cakes and donuts at meetings. Sometimes I indulge in whatever is out there. There is just something very comforting and enjoyable about sweets (and bad coffee) at a 12-Step meeting. They just seem to go hand in hand. And I don't feel guilty about it, either; nor should you, especially if you're just starting your sober journey. Sweets can be very important if you're brand new to sobriety. Your body has been living for so long on the sugar from alcohol that the cravings for sweets are going to be intense in the early days. So eat the damn donut and don't feel guilty about it.

The point is; **eating healthy doesn't mean we have to deny ourselves completely**. We can still enjoy fun food, but in moderation. As addicts, we need to recognize what is and isn't good for us and act accordingly and appropriately.

As you move forward in your recovery, try to keep a mental note of what kind of foods you're putting into your body every time you eat. You can even keep a food journal. Try to develop a conscious awareness of what kind of foods you eat and how often. Do you have a tendency to eat mostly processed or packaged food? Do you eat at fast food restaurants every day? What are you drinking, sodas or water? Do you eat fresh fruit every day?

The more aware you become about the food you're using to fuel your body-engine, the faster you'll recognize how to make adjustments that are beneficial, not harmful, to your body.

....

*Health Tip: *A food journal is a great way to track eating habits. Just keep a simple notepad with you, in your car or at home. Or you can create one on your phone or computer. Whatever is easiest usually works best. Write down what you eat each day. Don't worry about calories or fat content. Just get in the habit of tracking what you eat to give you a clear picture of the types of food you're consuming and how often.*

FOOD IS MEDICINE

Along with exercise and a healthy body weight, natural foods are essential to staying healthy, fighting disease and recovering from long term alcohol and drug addiction.

Certain foods reduce the risk of major health problems, including obesity, diabetes, heart disease and stroke. Others include intestinal disorders; irritable bowel syndrome; many forms of cancer; immune disorders including lupus; certain eye diseases; chronic kidney disease; chronic pain syndromes; and asthma. The typical American diet that is high in fat and low in fiber has been known to be a major contributor to obesity, diabetes and heart disease, largely because they promote excess weight.

So where can you turn to find a solution to all these nasty illnesses? Look no further than your kitchen for powerful disease fighters that can keep you healthy and strong for many years.

While a plant-based diet is ideal, limiting saturated fat by eating non-dairy products and lean cuts of meat will help reduce the amount of harmful components present in certain animal-based foods. It's important that we avoid, as often as possible, any junk food, high-fat meats, high-sugar foods, fast foods, and highly processed foods (most food that comes in a package or can is considered processed food).

10 Smart and Easy Eating Tips:

- ☑ Include a fresh fruit or vegetable with every meal.
- ☑ Enjoy a handful of nuts daily.
- ☑ Drink tea several times per day, especially green tea (we'll discuss this more later).
- ☑ Eat legumes like kidney beans, split peas and lentils three times per week.
- ☑ Eat whole-grain; browns rice, whole wheat pasta, quinoa, buckwheat, etc.
- ☑ Reduce the saturated fat content in recipes.
- ☑ Squeeze the juice of a lemon or lime into your water, beverages or foods.
- ☑ Go meatless three days per week (if you eat meat)
- ☑ Try "Meatless Mondays" and "Fish Fridays"
- ☑ Sprinkle a tablespoon of ground flax or chia seed into salads, yogurt and smoothies.
- ☑ Increase the amount of spices and herbs in your favorite recipes

A few simple adjustments can make a world of difference to your health. There are many ways to proceed beyond this list, but for now this is a good way to start.

TAKE IT EASY

One of the most common character defects we have as alcoholics and addicts is our desire for immediate gratification. We want and demand everything RIGHT NOW! We tend to be very impatient people. We're always in a hurry to get somewhere, even when we don't know where we want to go. We want it fast, and we want it now!

It's important to remember that sobriety is a journey, not a destination. In fact, all of life is a journey without any clear destination. All we have is today. We have to train ourselves to be calm and patient and enjoy each moment, even when every fiber in our body is screaming for an instant fix of some kind. We want everything yesterday and tomorrow's too late.

One of the best books I have ever read is called the "Power of Now" by Eckhart Tolle. I highly recommend it to anyone in recovery. It teaches, in a very clear and simple way, that our lives exist *in the moment,* and we should appreciate and enjoy each current experience without worrying about the past or the future.

This concept holds true in every part of your life, including your diet and health. It's important to take your time and remember that the world won't change in a single day. Learn to slow things down. Take it easy. The only thing that we can do is try to improve a little each day. Over time, the cumulative effects of our actions are what make the difference.

Remember, Rome wasn't built in a day. Nor will you rebuild your life in a day. Eat well. Exercise. Meditate. Go to 12-Step meetings. Hang out with family and friends you love and trust. Stay in the moment and let tomorrow arrive without worrying about the results of today's actions. Take it easy and enjoy the life, right here, right now.

....

*Quick Tip: *Read* The Power of Now*. If you're new to recovery, I highly recommend this book. It's simple to follow and profoundly insightful.*

PERFECTION

We often refer to certain people as a "perfectionist." Usually this refers to someone who is obsessive in their pursuits, refusing to accept any standard short of perfection.

Want to know the fastest way to drive yourself insane? Try being a perfectionist. The problem is you can never win. You can never reach your goal. You can never find or achieve perfection, because it doesn't exist.

When it comes to your health or sober journey, it's important to remember that there is no such thing as perfection. As the saying goes, *"perfection is the enemy of good."* There is only your best effort; and your best is good enough.

As addicts we're often very critical of ourselves (and certainly of others). We think that everything we do has to be better than anyone else can do it or else it's a complete failure. The truth is we tend to have narcissistic personalities. We're born believing that we're extremely special, gifted and unique and that everything we do is important and deserving of recognition and praise. We expect a trophy every time we pass gas. As we get older, reality sets in and we discover that our cosmic awesomeness is more of a self-created myth. Unfortunately, we usually cling to the idea that if we just work obsessively enough at something, we will achieve the perfect outcome and our lives, and the universe, will all make sense again.

But this type of obsessive focus usually results in disappointment. We will never, ever achieve perfection in anything we do. Perfection is for God, not humans.

When we set out to achieve a goal, like improving our health or maintaining our sobriety, it's important to always remember that we can and should do our very best each day. But it's equally important to remember that we're imperfect and make mistakes. Some days we're great, some days we're mediocre, some days we completely screw things up. However, as long as we're giving it our best shot each time, we're always succeeding. *Success is in the effort, not just the result.*

What does all this have to do with your health and nutrition journey? The effort you put into it every day is what matters most. You're not going to be perfect at this. Do your best, forget the rest.

- ☑ *Try* to eat healthy every day
- ☑ *Try* to exercise daily
- ☑ *Try* to get enough sleep
- ☑ *Try* to relax or meditate each day
- ☑ *Try* to learn about your body and what makes it healthy

Try every day, but don't get discouraged if the results you seek don't happen immediately. Your health recovery is similar to your addiction recovery; take it one day at a time, forget about doing it perfectly because no one ever has or ever will. Go easy on yourself and leave perfection to God.

....

***Quick Tip**: *Learning how to embrace our own flaws and imperfections is not only liberating, it can also be empowering. Try to be more self-deprecating. When you make a mistake or screw up, remember it's not the end of the world. Lighten up and learn to laugh at yourself sometimes.*

OVEREATING; BE CAREFUL, BE SMART

When we give up one addiction, it's easy to quickly replace it with another addiction. Too often people get sober only to replace their addiction to alcohol or drugs with addiction to food or sex. This book is not about sex (sorry) so we're going to focus on the food part.

Much like addiction to alcohol, I think that over-eating is another form of addiction manifesting in a different way with a different substance. We have to be careful how far we take it and monitor our obsessions. Every time I picked up a drink the addiction would quickly take over and the craving for more became so overwhelming and obsessive (known as the "*phenomenon of craving*") that I had no choice but to continue drinking until I passed out or ran out of booze.

I've often struggled with the same intense craving when it comes to food, especially food that has a lot of sugar. I absolutely love sweets. And I enjoy eating them to this day. *Cookies and cakes and ice cream, oh my!* However, I'm also aware that if I'm not careful, I will eat sweets around the clock, and it will quickly show up on my waistline.

In many ways, food is like alcohol. For some people, food (like alcohol) brings great comfort and relief from the daily burdens, stress and pain of life. Unhealthy foods—fast-food, greasy food, salty food, processed food—seem to be the most popular choice when it comes to seeking comfort through excessive eating. Let's be honest, you won't find a lot of obese people stuffing their faces with organic apples, carrots and celery then washing it all down with an ice cold glass of spring water. Obese people, or those who will become obese, usually reach for the heaviest, greasiest, saltiest food available.

Food can be very comforting and soothing to the soul, temporarily anyway. So if one bite—like one drink—makes you feel better, why not have two, then three? Why stop at all when it makes you feel so much better?

Be careful and be wise when it comes to what you eat and how often. Make smart food choices every day. Most importantly, try not to transfer one addiction over to another addiction.

....

*Health Tip: The standard way to eat in our culture is three large meals per day. This can often lead to filling up on too much food all at once. Instead of eating three large meals every day, try eating five small meals spread out across the entire day. It will help your digestion and you won't feel so bloated after each meal.

AGUA, BABY!

Remember those horrendous hangovers you suffered through all the time? The kind where you wake up feeling like a dried up turd that's been baking in the sun? Your mouth is dry and tastes like hell warmed over. Your teeth feel like they're wearing wool sweaters. Your throat burns. Your head is pounding. Your eyes are stinging. Those mornings where you crawl out of bed and have to chug a half gallon of water because you're so parched you feel brittle.

I remember clearly how awful it felt opening my eyes every morning (or afternoon) to confront the pain and suffering of daily hangovers. Alcohol dehydrates the body significantly. Thus, the day after we drink we're as dry as sand paper.

One of the most important things we can do to maintain our health is to keep a steady flow of water passing through our bodies. Every single cell in your body requires water to function properly. Your internal organs, skin, and hair all require an abundance of clean water.

As you've probably already heard, up to 60% of the human body is made of water. Look at these statistics to get a clear understanding of the water content in an average adult body:

- ☑ The brain is composed of 73% water
- ☑ The heart is composed of 73% water
- ☑ The lungs are composed of 83% water
- ☑ The bones are composed of 31% water
- ☑ The skin is composed of 64% water
- ☑ The muscles are composed of 79% water
- ☑ The kidneys are composed of 79% water

That's a lot of water, boys and girls! But all that water has to come from somewhere, and it ain't from eating cheeseburgers. Your muscles in particular need water in order to strengthen and grow. Every part of your body needs water to thrive.

It's crucial to your body to keep it flowing in order to keep it going!

Keep water with you all the time. Not just when you're exercising. Carry a bottle with you to work, to the store, to school, to every place you go. Keep water by your bedside and by your TV. The more water you drink the healthier you will look and feel.

....

Health Tip: Health professionals recommend the "8x8 rule" which suggests we drink eight ounces of water eight times per day. Buy an eight ounce drinking container and fill it eight times each day starting in the morning and ending an hour before bed.

FROM THE DIRT

I f you want to supercharge your health, eat from the dirt.
It's amazing to me how our planet has been
designed to produce the healthiest foods we can eat,
in great abundance, directly from the soil. It's aston-
ishing when you think about how we can simply mix
a few seeds with dirt and water then in a short time
we're given plants and fruit that can sustain all life on
the planet. That simple fact alone deepens my faith in
a Higher Power, a Creator that provides nourishment
from almost every corner of the earth. Miraculous!

Think about it. Just the process of an apple coming to fruition is a miracle. It starts as a seed that is
married to the soil. Then its fed *water* (the plants need
water as much as humans). As it grows out of the soil
it reaches for the sun which provides energy, fueling its
growth. Eventually the sapling becomes a tree which
then gives birth to APPLES.

We usually don't put much thought into where our
fruits and vegetables come from, but a little research
and study paints a picture of something that occurs all
day, every day, everywhere on the planet.

What's most important to remember is that the food that comes directly from the soil, like fruits, vegetables, seeds, grains and legumes, are crucial to your long-term health. Being told to eat your vegetables as a child wasn't a hoax being forced on you as some kind of cruel joke. It was a suggestion based in fact.

As I stated earlier, *you are what you eat.* The vast majority of your vitamins, nutrients and energy are going to come directly from natural (preferably organic) plant-based food. Make it a point to eat an abundance of these foods every day if you can. If you don't have immediate access to fresh produce daily, try to incorporate them as often as you can whenever the opportunity arises. Fresh fruit in particular can be easy to find and is often sweet enough to replace synthetic sweets like donuts and candy bars.

....

*Health Tip: There are numerous drinks made from fruits and vegetables that are available just about everywhere. Products like V8 Juice, Naked Juice and Suja Juice are a quick and easy way to load up of the nutrients that come from produce. There are also many juice bars and smoothie shops in most towns and cities. But don't rely on these products exclusively because they can have high levels of natural sugars and sodium (salt).

SUPERFOODS

I n the simplest terms, superfoods are natural, nutrient-dense foods that supply your body with everything it needs to function at the highest level. For a food to be in the 'Super' category, it needs to be a power hitter in the antioxidant and anti-inflammatory category, carrying with it the ability to protect your heart from damaging free radicals. High levels of free radicals cause inflammation and irritation in our arteries and vessels that cause hearts attack and strokes. In addition to being high in antioxidant vitamins and minerals, Superfoods are also a good source of fiber that helps keep arteries clear and lower cholesterol numbers.

As you embark on your new health journey, add these foods to your shopping list and experiment with them in recipes and meals or enjoy them as snacks.

☑ **Green Leafy Vegetables**—By adding more veggies to your diet, you increase the volume of foods eaten while reducing calorie intake.

☑ **Apples**—The crunch in apples signal our brain that we're satisfied and the natural sugars in fruit come loaded with fiber and antioxidants that make a perfect swap for processed sweets.

☑ **Nuts**—Nuts are packed with healthy protein, healthy fat, and are nutrient-dense.

☑ **Beans and Legumes** - A great source of healthy carbs and proteins, they're high in fiber and slow down digestion, helping us stay full longer.

☑ **Eggs**—Healthy protein helps us feel full and regulates hunger and fullness signals. Limit to seven whole eggs in a week to stay heart fit.

☑ **Yogurt**—Protein-packed, full of probiotics that promote gut health and weight loss, high in calcium, and a source of healthy carbs. Choose yogurt with limited or no sugar.

☑ **Salmon**—All forms of fish offer healthy protein, and fatty fishes like salmon, tuna, sardines and mackerel provide an abundance of nutrients.

☑ **Whole grains**—While fad diets are giving all grains a bad rap, whole grains provide an important source of fiber, B vitamins (thiamin, riboflavin, niacin and folate) and many minerals (phosphorus, zinc, copper, iron, magnesium and selenium), thus making them healthy carbs. They're also shown to reduce the risk of obesity, so include modest portions multiple times daily. Choices include whole-grain bread products, oats, quinoa, brown/ black/red/wild rice, barley, and wheat berries.

☑ **Chia Seeds**—A great source of healthy fat and fiber, these seeds help stabilize energy and mood. Add to most any meal for a nutritious boost.

☑ **Berries**—all berries types are loaded with Flavonoids and Vitamin C, and high in fiber. Blend them into smoothies, eat in equal parts with yogurt or eat them as a snack.

☑ **Flax seed**—Each tablespoon of ground flaxseed contains about 1.8 grams of plant Omega-3s as well as antioxidants.

☑ **Kale**—A very good source of Vitamin A, Vitamin C, Vitamin K, Vitamin B6, and Potassium, as well as Copper and Manganese. Consume raw in salads, or stir fry or steam with other vegetables. If you don't like the taste (like me) blend into smoothies.

☑ **Almonds & Walnuts**—Nutrients include Vitamin E, Copper and Magnesium. Grab a handful daily for a high fiber, healthy fat and protein.

☑ **Broccoli**—High in fiber, Vitamin E, Manganese, and Carotenoids. Enjoy raw or cooked.

☑ **Avocado**—Technically a fruit, avocados contain over 20 vitamins and minerals essential for heart health. Go easy on these, however because they're loaded with monounsaturated fat. A quarter to half of an avocado is a reasonable portion.

☑ **Cherries**—A cup provides 16% of the recommended vitamin C for the day. Not in season? Frozen or canned (avoid canned in heavy syrup as sugar is pro-inflammatory) have all the nutritional value of fresh cherries.

☑ **Sweet Potatoes**—An excellent source of vitamin A, vitamin C, Manganese, Copper, Pantothenic acid and Vitamin B6.

☑ **Citrus**—Load up on Vitamin C and Lycopene with oranges and grapefruit, and squeeze the juice of lemons and limes **into your water** each day to establish a heart-healthy routine of drinking 'super water'.

....

__Health Tip:__ Make a copy of this list of superfoods and tape it to your refrigerator so you'll have it front of you every time you reach for something to eat.

LEAN MEAN PROTEIN

The human body needs protein, and lots of it. Protein builds and repairs muscles, bones, tissues, cartilage, blood and skin as well as making enzymes and hormones that you need to survive. If you're new to sobriety or just to trying to build strength, protein is the essential component that you need to add to your diet every day.

There seems to be a never-ending debate about animal protein versus plant-based protein, and which is better, healthier and more ethical. On the one side are the meat eaters who are convinced that humans need to eat animal protein because we've been eating it for thousands of years and our bodies require it at this stage of our evolution. On the other side are the vegetarians and vegans who feel that we can get all the protein we need from a wide variety of plant-based foods so there's no need to keep killing other species that inhabit earth.

It's a debate that probably won't ever be resolved, at least not in my life time. When it comes to my personal opinion on the subject, I fall somewhere between the two camps. I've tried vegetarianism and veganism several times. My wife and I managed to go completely whole-food, plant based for an entire year once. But ultimately we found it too difficult and eventually began to slowly reincorporate certain animal proteins back into our diet.

I will say that eating a strictly plant-based diet has its benefits. We both felt great at first. We lost a little weight and had fun experimenting with new vegan recipes. But eventually we became bored with it and craved certain types of animal protein, fish and eggs in particular. In my opinion (and this is just an opinion), I found eating a strictly plant-based diet to be somewhat dull and repetitive. I also felt that I was losing muscle strength and becoming lethargic.

These days I try to maintain an 80/20 rule; I try to eat 80% plant-based food and 20% animal protein. Mostly I eat fruits, vegetables and grains with a small amount of animal protein, usually with dinner.

Typically, I have a small amount of chicken, fish or eggs each day. Personally, I never eat red meat. If you choose to eat red meat, try to eat organic, grass fed beef in limited amounts, perhaps once per week or once per month.

Lean, organic protein is your best bet if you want to include animal protein in your diet. Free range chicken, fresh wild-caught fish, organic eggs and lean organic turkey are all healthy and easy to cook. Try to always buy **organic, natural products,** not packaged or processed which tend to have more chemicals and preservatives added.

There are numerous plants that provide an abundance of protein as well, including:

- ☑ Soy products
- ☑ Lentils
- ☑ Chickpeas
- ☑ Nuts
- ☑ Spirulina
- ☑ Quinoa
- ☑ Chia seeds
- ☑ Hemp seeds
- ☑ Beans
- ☑ Potatoes
- ☑ Dark leafy greens (like kale)
- ☑ Seitan

Wherever you fall on the debate between plant and animal protein, find what works best and make sure to include plenty of protein in your diet every day. Keep it lean and mean and your body will thank you for the gift

....

*Health Tip: *There are a variety of protein powders that you can blend into smoothies, juices, yogurt or oatmeal that are available in any natural food store. They tend to be expensive, but can provide a quick and easy blast of protein each morning or as a midday snack.*

SUPPLEMENTS

I believe that we should get the majority of our essential nutrients and vitamins directly from the food we eat. If we're eating a diet that consists of primarily fresh, organic fruits, vegetables and lean protein, our bodies will thrive and our health will improve. However, there are times when I think certain supplements can contribute to our health journey and speed up the process, especially when recovering from years of substance abuse and an unhealthy, sedentary lifestyle.

When I first got sober, one of my favorite things to do was visit the local health food stores in my city, exploring the wide variety of exotic supplements filling the shelves (*a much more rewarding activity than exploring the local liquor stores shelves*). At the time I was living in Los Angeles, which has an abundance of health food stores. It's ironic that a city like Los Angeles can provide so many toxic substances to feed our addictions while at the same time (and often on the same corner) offering so many healthy options that can improve our health. It all comes down to the choices we make.

In the early months of my recovery I experimented with a host of vitamins and supplements. There are endless choices it seems, and they can be quite pricey. Vitamins and supplements can be expensive. So the best approach I found was to keep it to the simple list I have provided below. Most importantly, for safety reasons never buy any vitamins or supplements that are made in China, India or any country other than the United States, Canada or Western Europe where manufacturing regulations are generally strict. In order to get started, consider the following:

- ☑ **Multi Vitamins**—A good multivitamin should be the cornerstone of your supplement plan. I recommend a daily multivitamin to anyone who is new to recovery. Find one that offers a large blend of essential nutrients and vitamins. My favorite is *Nature Made*, but there are many to choose from with a variety of prices that you can find in any grocery store or online.
- ☑ **Vitamin C**—Essential for the repair and growth of every body tissue
- ☑ **Fish Oil**—Get your daily dose of Omega-3's. One of the best things you can take every day is a small dose of natural, organic fish oil. Helps with heart health, digestion, skin and hair repair, liver function and supports weight loss.

☑ **Non-Flush Niacin**—I took this for high cholesterol. Within a few months my cholesterol
was back to normal. Be careful of taking regular Niacin (versus non-flush) which may causes
face flushing and hot flashes. I tried it once and
it sucked. So stick with the non-flush variety.

☑ **Natural Sleep Aid**—I first began using
plant-based sleep aids in early recovery and
still use them today when I'm struggling to
get a full night of sleep. Many people like to
take Melatonin, which you might like, but it
makes me very groggy in the morning and
gives me a slight headache. I prefer *Wild
Harvest Sleep Better*, which helps me sleep
soundly with no after effects.

These are just a few suggestions that have worked
for me over the years, particularly in early recovery. If
you're able to find a good supplement store or natural
food store in your area, explore the aisles and learn all
you can. You can also pick up an enormous amount of
information on the internet.

⋯⋯⋯⋯⋯⋯⋯⋯⋯⋯⋯⋯⋯⋯⋯⋯⋯⋯⋯⋯⋯⋯⋯⋯⋯⋯⋯⋯⋯

*Health Tip: *If you are on a fixed or limited budget, just find one
multivitamin and skip all the others for now. Take one daily in
the morning and remember to make wise food choices throughout
each day to ensure you're feeding your body all the natural vitamins and nutrients it requires.*

HERBAL TEAS

ike vitamins, enjoying daily herbal teas can have a very healthy and calming effect on your body. I still enjoy drinking coffee every morning. But I also incorporate tea into my life often. When I first got sober I drank tea all the time and enjoyed the benefits of the many tea varieties that are available.

Again, your local health food store or grocery store will have many herbal teas to explore and try. There seems to be an herbal tea for just about everything imaginable; liver health, digestion, constipation, muscle aches, anxiety, energy, nausea, allergies, heartburn, sleep… If there's a human ailment, there's an herbal tea for it.

Herbal teas are enjoyable and come in a wide variety of interesting flavors and fragrances. There's a reason why herbal teas are so immensely popular around the world; they're delicious, soothing and healthy. Add honey or stevia, and they become a sweet treat any time of day.

A few favorites:

☑ English Breakfast

☑ Earl Grey
☑ Darjeeling
☑ Green Tea
☑ White Tea
☑ Oolong
☑ Jasmine
☑ Chamomile
☑ Sleepy Time

Green tea, in particular, has very powerful health benefits that should not be ignored. The nutrients and compounds in green tea are known to be helpful to your body. If you were to choose only one kind of tea to drink, green tea is the one to pick. Do yourself a favor and start drinking green tea every day.

....

*Health Tip: *Green tea is incredibly healthy for you. Drink it daily hot or cold. Make a large batch of honey-sweetened iced green tea and bring a bottle wherever you go.*

SMOOTHIES

One of my favorite words in the English language is… VITAMIX®. Just the sound of that word conjures up visions of delicious, nutritious green smoothies, tropical smoothies, and banana chocolate smoothies. If you think that blenders are only for mixing margaritas and daiquiris, think again.

A Vitamix® is an incredibly powerful machine that will pulverize and blend just about any food you throw into it. Most importantly, it offers a fast and efficient way to consolidate multiple ingredients into a single drink that will supercharge your health. There are, of course, other blender options available that are less expensive. But as far as I can find, the Vitamix® does the best job and will survive in your kitchen for years. Whether you choose a Vitamix® or another brand, it's a worthwhile investment to buy a good blender and start experimenting with smoothies.

If you feel lazy, tired or just don't want to spend any amount of time preparing meals or cooking (or don't know how to cook), then smoothies are by far the best way for you to pack your breakfast, lunch or dinner with everything you need to fuel your body. Smoothies can be stuffed with multiple green vegetables then sweetened with just about any fruit you can get your hands on; apples, bananas, mangos, pears, pineapples, papaya all work great. Load your smoothies with fresh organic fruits and vegetables, nuts and seeds, oatmeal, yogurt and many other things that are healthy and taste good.

At the end of this book are listed several smoothie recipes that you might enjoy. If you're brand new to recovery, or just want to improve your health, consider smoothies as one of the easiest and most effective methods to reach your goal.

....

*__Health Tip__: *There are many organic protein powders you can add to your smoothies that will increase their potency. A few brands you might enjoy include Orgain, Garden of Life, and Organifi. You can also add apple, orange or pineapple juice to sweeten things up.*

GET JUICED

I was fairly new to sobriety when my friend, Henry, turned me on to the concept of juicing. He was also in the early stages of recovery and began sharing his experience with juicing, expressing how effective it was at improving his overall health, in particular the condition of his skin and hair, and the tremendous amount of energy he was enjoying.

I was skeptical at first but eventually decided to give juicing a try. As I mentioned earlier, my skin was still in pretty bad shape from all the years of substance abuse, and my energy level was pretty low most days. I figured I had nothing to lose.

I bought an inexpensive juicer and began squeezing out daily concoctions made from apples, celery, lettuce, carrots, lemons, ginger and a wide variety of other vegetables and fruits. First and foremost, I absolutely loved how fresh juice tasted. It was a shock to my senses. Each drink I made was sweet, aromatic and earthy.

After a few days of juicing I definitely noticed an uptick in my energy level, especially whenever I drank a fresh batch first thing in the morning. And my skin began to have more color and was less dry. Eventually, I also began to lose weight the more I juiced.

Juicing is a simple way to flood your body with nutrients fresh from the source. Granted, you will sacrifice some of the fiber that comes from eating whole foods (smoothies retain their fiber content). But there is no doubt that you can and will retain a very large amount of vitamins, nutrients and minerals that your body craves. Fresh juices are also an anti-inflammatory and can boost your immune system to fight sickness and disease. Additionally, regular juicing will improve digestion and elimination.

Some people get frustrated by juicing because of the clean-up involved after making a batch. But in my opinion it's worth the extra effort to reap the rewards of consuming sweet, natural juices made from fresh fruits and vegetables.

---

*Health Tip: *Make a large batch of juice in the morning, and keep part of it in the refrigerator for an energy boost in the afternoon. Or take some with you in a large sports bottle to sip throughout the day.*

PART THREE

MOVE IT OR LOSE IT

*It is a shame for a man to grow old without
seeing the beauty and strength
of which his body is capable.*
~ Socrates

SHAKE, RATTLE AND ROLL

Does the word "exercise" fill you with dread? When you hear the term "working out" do you suddenly panic and start looking for the nearest escape route to freedom? If you're like most recovering addicts, the idea of exercising is as appealing as brain surgery: *"No, thanks; I'll just enjoy the aneurysm, thank you very much."*

As addicts, we prefer the easy way whenever possible. We seek the path of least resistance, even if the path we're on is self-destructive. In many ways, it's why we drink and use. We prefer the fastest, easiest route to feeling good (or not feeling anything at all). **We want immediate gratification and the idea of working hard for what we truly want or need goes against our nature.**

But exercise doesn't have to be feared or avoided. Rather, it should be welcomed and embraced. Exercise doesn't have to be difficult, either. In fact, some of the most effective forms of exercise are easy and very enjoyable.

I know from my own experience that working out and exercise were the farthest thing from my mind when I was still drinking and using. My idea of exercise was lifting a twelve ounce can of beer, chopping up a line of coke, then quickly lighting a cigarette while talking my head off to anyone who was unfortunate enough to be stuck in the same room with me. This was my version of going to the gym. By the time I finally got sober, I was a flabby, wheezing mess. I looked and felt like Jabba the Hutt with a hangover.

When I was new to recovery I needed to find the easiest form of exercise possible, otherwise I knew I wouldn't stick with it. So I began to walk. At first I just walked around the block once a day. Then I started walking to my 12-Step meetings (luckily, there were several in my Los Angeles neighborhood). I would walk to the store, to meet friends, to get coffee. I walked as often as I could. It felt great, and most importantly it cleared my head and gave me small shots of peace and contentment. I truly started enjoying walking and looked forward to it every day. Eventually, within a few months, I was doing a combination of *walking, hiking, and jogging* every day and the weight was melting away.

The point I want to emphasize is that I had to start moving!

If you've been living an addiction lifestyle, most likely you've been abusing and neglecting your body in many subtle and not so subtle ways. If you've been living on a steady diet of booze, drugs, cigarettes and poor food choices, combined with a sedentary lifestyle, than you need to get up off the couch and shake, rattle and roll your body to get it back into shape. You don't have to run a marathon or become a champion weight lifter. You just have to start moving your body in a few simple, enjoyable ways (I will provide numerous ideas in the following pages).

Exercise doesn't have to fill you with dread nor make you run for the door. The only thing you need to do is find an activity that you enjoy and that elevates your heart rate and pushes your muscles a little at a time. Start simple and experiment with various forms of exercise, and before you know it, you'll start feeling better, sleeping well, losing weight and loving your life again.

....

*Health Tip: *Take a short walk every morning. It doesn't have to be long, just 10 minutes to start. Walk to the store or to the mailbox, whatever. Just get up and walk first thing in the morning to move your feet, get the blood flowing, and smell the fresh morning air. And if you have a friend who also wants to improve their health, form a support team and start walking and exercising together.*

CARDIO HEALTH

One of the most common forms of damage from long term addiction is the damage we inflict on our heart and lungs. If you've spent years smoking cigarettes, weed, crack or meth, then most likely your lungs and heart are begging for mercy. The same is true with drinking, which when taken to extremes, has a direct, negative impact on your entire cardio system.

Your heart and lungs are just like every other muscle or organ in your body. If you neglect or abuse them, they begin to lose strength. If we're not loyal to our bodies, our bodies will not be loyal in return. Most of us go years without any proper cardio exercise (*Sorry, but running up the stairs to your dealer's apartment doesn't count as exercise*).

You have to do something, ANYTHING, to exercise your cardio system! You have to get moving!

When I first got sober I had a very distinct, high pitched wheezing noise that came from my lungs. It was pathetic and a little scary. I could barely walk more than a few blocks without feeling an ache in my chest, as if I was running a marathon. I would sweat just walking across my apartment. Walking up a hill was so uncomfortable I simply avoided it all together— *nothing but flat surfaces for me, thank you.* There were times I had to pause and bend over to catch my breath from doing the most mundane things like taking out the garbage or getting in and out of the shower. I was a mess and my lungs and heart let me know every step.

It was obvious that I had sustained significant damage to my cardio system. What I quickly learned, however, was that the damage could be reversed fairly quickly. What was required of me, and of you, is exercising the heart and lungs through simple cardio activities every day. It doesn't have to be complicated. Just get up and start moving your body in a way that you enjoy. We'll review a few ideas in the upcoming pages.

....

Health Tip: STOP SMOKING, DAMN IT!

WALK IT OFF

Now that we're sober, the term "*walk it off*" has an entirely new meaning. Before, we had to "*walk off*" the effects of being too drunk on any given night. Now we have to "*walk off*" the long term effects of being drunk over many years. In order for us to get our health back we need to start moving, and walking is the best way to start.

We discussed walking earlier, but it bears repeating. Walking (assuming you have the ability to walk) is the easiest and most immediate exercise routine you have available to you. It's like having your own personal gym that's open twenty four hours per day. And it's very effective, too. There's no reason why you shouldn't be walking every day, preferably several times per day.

You don't have to walk 20 miles at a time, either. Just go outside and walk for 10 or 15 minutes in the morning. Then do it a few more times that day.

Walking is great for rebuilding your leg and back muscles. The system of movement your body engages in when you walk has a positive effect on your entire physical structure, including your arms, shoulders, heart and lungs. It's also great for relieving stress and anxiety, which is beneficial to your mental and spiritual health.

If you can walk somewhere instead of driving than you should walk. If you need to go to the store, and its close enough, walk there. If there's a 12-Step meeting close to your home, walk to the meeting. If you have a friend who is elderly or lonely, be of service by asking them if they want to take a short walk. If you have children, take them for a walk as an excuse to spend time with them. If you have a dog, take him or her for a long walk every day. If you have a cat, you can try putting a harness on him or her and taking a walk (but please don't blame me if people laugh at you).

Walking is easy and enjoyable and will help you get back into shape. It's also a wonderful way to clear your head, collect your thoughts, and diminish stress and anxiety. So don't wait for a perfect day or time or perfect weather (walking in the rain and snow has its own form of pleasure). Get started today. *And if you decide to take your cat for a walk, please take a photograph and send it to me. I can always use a good laugh.*

....

Quick Tip: Buy earphones for your cell phone so you can listen to music while you walk. But be aware of traffic and your surroundings. Keep the volume low enough that you know what's happening around you at all times.

STRETCHING

You know that wonderful feeling you get every time you stretch your arms over your head when you wake up in the morning? It feels great and can bring a smile to our face. If something feels that good, why not repeat it as a part of your daily exercise routine?

Stretching is very good for you and shouldn't be ignored. This is true for anyone at any age, but it's particularly true if you're middle aged or older. There is certainly nothing complicated about stretching, and it can be done anywhere, in any room of your house. You can even stretch in the shower while the warm water helps loosen and relax tight muscles.

Stretching can increase your flexibility, improve posture and reduce certain aches and pains, especially in the back and shoulders. Equally important, stretching can reduce stress. In the next section we'll discuss yoga, which is simply a more elevated and intense form of stretching. But to get started, keep it simple and try to stretch first thing in the morning or just before you exercise.

Benefits of stretching include:

- ☑ Greater range of motion
- ☑ Reduced stress and anxiety
- ☑ Calms the mind
- ☑ Improves athletic performance
- ☑ Improves posture
- ☑ Can reduce back and shoulder pain
- ☑ Can reduce tension headaches
- ☑ Feels amazing

Try to develop a ten minute stretching routine each morning. There are numerous web sites, Youtube videos and books that will illustrate a variety of easy stretching techniques for you to try. It doesn't take a major commitment to incorporate stretching into your day, and the benefits will far out weight the minimal effort required from you.

....

*****Health Tip:** *If you have back or weight problems, try stretching while seated in a stable chair. There are plenty of seated stretching routines that you can find online that are as effective and enjoyable as any other form of stretching.*

DANCE IF YOU DARE

For many people who are new to recovery, learning how to dance sober is as scary as learning how to have sober sex. Both seem equally frightening after years of relying on alcohol to give you the courage to "move," either in bed or on the dance floor.

The fact is, dancing is not only fun it can also be a great form of exercise (*by the way, the same is true with sex, but that's a subject for another book*). Dancing is a great way to move your body, tone your legs and improve your cardio strength. It's also a great way to work up a sweat and drop some weight. Dancing also releases endorphins in your brain, which helps elevate your mood and can often diminish depression and anxiety.

Not everyone enjoys dancing, either sober or drunk, and I admit it's not my favorite pastime either. I still struggle with shyness and social discomfort, so dancing can still be a challenge for me in a crowd of people. But when I was newly sober I discovered that I could put my favorite music on, crank up the volume, and dance my ass off ALONE in my apartment. And it was a blast! I know it sounds goofy and sort of dorky, and it was! Just the image of a bloated, fat, forty three year old recovering addict dancing alone in his apartment makes me laugh when I think about it. *Thank God there is no video that exists of those silly moments dancing with myself.*

But in truth, it was actually pretty damn fun. And it turned out to be a great form of exercise. I didn't care what I looked like when I was dancing or how ridiculous it might've seemed. What mattered was I was moving and grooving, sweating up a storm, listening to great music and actually having a great time dancing. I prefer rock 'n roll and blues, but I also tried out a bunch of other music styles just to keep things interesting and new.

Seriously, give dancing a try. Men in particular are often reluctant to dance sober. It just feels so damn awkward without a head full of booze or coke. But it's worth trying and dancing brings enormous health benefits. And if you feel foolish doing it, that's okay. Just lock the doors, close the blinds, crank up the volume and move, baby! No one needs to know what you're up to. This is for you, not anyone else. And don't be surprised if you catch yourself smiling from ear to ear as you begin to groove.

....

Health Tip: On some days you can replace your walks with dancing, especially if it's raining or snowing outside. Put on headphones to really get the full impact of the music and let your feet fly.

THE MIRACLE CALLED YOGA

There really is nothing quite like yoga for mind, body and spiritual health. Yoga is a great form of exercise and offers many proven techniques for relaxing your mind and calming your spirit. I would highly recommend it to anyone looking to improve their health. Most importantly, there are many forms of yoga for every level of experience. If you've never tried it before there are many easy forms of yoga you can try, including chair or seated yoga that can be practiced by just about anyone who is willing to try and learn. No matter what physical shape you're in, you can find a form of yoga that will fit your capabilities.

If you've never attempted yoga before, it's time to start. Yes, I know it looks difficult and awkward, but yoga is one of the best things you can do for your body and mind in the recovery of your health. There are yoga classes for beginners in every community in the United States. Start with a simple "gentle yoga" style class, and you will be amazed at how good it feels.

During the early days of my sobriety, I was in terrible physical shape. I slowly started to improve my health by taking long walks every day. Eventually, I joined a local gym and started jogging on the treadmill and lifting weights. A friend suggested I add yoga into my workout routine, which at the time, sounded ridiculous. To my way of thinking, taking a yoga class was the same as taking a ballet class (*not that there's anything wrong with that*).

But my friend was persistent so eventually I gave in and joined a beginner class at my gym.

I have to admit, my first few attempts at yoga were pretty pathetic. My body was stiffer than a frozen pretzel. I could barely stretch. But I discovered that after each class, even when it was difficult, my entire body felt relaxed. And yoga seemed to supply me with energy and a more positive mood. I quickly became a yoga addict (not all addictions are bad).

One of the best aspects of yoga is the fact that it lends itself so well to meditation. In fact, yoga is its own form of meditation.

Some of the proven benefits of yoga include:

- ☑ Improved your state of mind
- ☑ Reduced depression and anxiety
- ☑ Improved your flexibility
- ☑ Builds overall muscle strength in your entire body
- ☑ Improved your posture
- ☑ Reduced back pain

☑ Protects your spine
☑ Increased blood flow throughout your entire
   body

Once you've learned the basics and are able to get past any feelings of awkwardness, the flow of yoga is a great way to practice mindfulness (meditation). If you focus all your attention on each movement, pose, and your breath, then your mind will quiet down. You will become completely immersed in the yoga.

Yoga is a great form of exercise and will improve your physical fitness. Combined with its intrinsic meditative qualities, yoga is a smart choice for just about everyone.

....

*Health Tip: *If you're completely new to yoga, start with a beginner lesson, sometimes called "gentle yoga." If you feel self-conscious about joining a class, there are numerous online videos that will teach you the basics of yoga so you can learn in the privacy of your home.*

INTO NATURE WE GO

When you think about it, hiking is just walking on a slant. There's certainly nothing complicated about it, it just requires a little more effort to walk up hill. But that uphill effort is what makes it even more effective than just walking on a flat surface. Once you get to a point in your health recovery, when you feel like you're getting back into some degree of shape, it might be a good idea to "step up" your exercise routine by incorporating a short hike or two into your week.

Hiking is great for every part of your body including your leg muscles (your calves in particular), back muscles, stomach and side muscles, as well as your cardio condition. You will probably notice that it takes a shorter period of time to feel fatigue and muscle tension in your body, especially your legs, when you first start hiking. And you'll probably feel out of breath faster as well. The uphill angle adds a greater degree of pressure and difficulty to your body, more than walking does. But that's the point. You want to start increasing your strength and endurance and hiking is a great way to start.

Equally important, hiking gives you an opportunity to explore the outdoors beyond your neighborhood. Getting out into nature is one of the best gifts you can give yourself. The air is generally cleaner, the views and scenery are more beautiful, and it provides the perfect setting to clear your mind and release stress, depression and anxiety.

When I was a few months sober, I tried walking up a very long, steep trail in Los Angeles called Runyon Canyon. For people who live in LA, it's a well-known and popular spot, frequented by celebrities and outdoor enthusiasts. Los Angeles may not be the first place you think of when you think about nature, but this specific spot is quite beautiful and offers amazing panoramic views of the city from the top.

The trail up Runyon Canyon is only about 2.5 miles. However it's a steep climb and can be challenging to anyone who isn't in decent shape. When I first attempted to climb Runyon, it was EXHAUSTING! I somehow managed to make it to the top very slowly by willpower alone, stopping many times along the way while drinking a ton of water (*always bring water on any hike*). But I finally made it to the top and was extremely proud of my accomplishment, as if I'd made it to the top of Mount Everest. And here is the best part: I kept at it and started climbing it once per week. Within three months I could climb it with ease. Within six months I was able to jog (very slowly) to the top without stopping. Remember that movie scene in *Titanic* when Jack stands at the bow of the ship with his arms out screaming *"I'm the king of the world!"* Well, that was me after I jogged to the top of Runyon. I felt like the king of the world, able to accomplish anything.

Jogging to the top of Runyon Canyon still remains one of my greatest achievements in early sobriety. It meant so much to me then and still fills me with pride today, almost 12 years later. To go from an overweight, cigarette-pounding, burger-scarfing, alcohol-addicted, coke-snorting couch potato to jogging from the base to the top of Runyon Canyon was a great day for me, and I still carry that memory fondly in my heart (*a much healthier heart today*).

However, the truth is, it took time. It didn't happen overnight. And it won't happen instantly for you either. **But you have to start pushing yourself a little harder every day**. By adding an easy, enjoyable hike into your routine once per week, you will be on your way to a much healthier body, mind and spirit.

....

Health Tip: In addition to bringing water on every hike, buy a good pair of hiking shoes or sneakers that are comfortable and offer good support. Good shoes aren't inexpensive, but they're well worth the investment over time.

THE RUNNER'S "HIGH"

When we talk about huffing and puffing, we're not talking about inhaling glue from a paper bag or smoking crack from a glass pipe. Leave that to the junkies who are still out there using and dying. What we're talking about, as *recovering* addicts, is elevating our cardio exercise to the next level, *huffing and puffing* while jogging or running.

I know, I know… The idea of jogging sounds like as much as fun as hitting yourself repeatedly in the forehead with a hammer. But it's not as bad as it sounds if you start slowly and work yourself up to longer distances over time.

You've probably heard people refer to the "runner's high." As a recovering addict, maybe that will get you excited enough to try jogging. Essentially, the "runner's high" is a strong feeling of euphoria (listen up, cokeheads) coupled with reduced anxiety and a lessened ability to feel pain. Sound familiar? Isn't that what we've all been chasing anyway? So why not try getting high naturally, using your own body's ability to produce endorphins through exercise?

For some people, jogging simply isn't possible due to physical restrictions such as knee or back injuries. If that's the case, you can stick with walking and hiking, just add more time and distance. But jogging is a very good way to excel physically and will have a mighty impact on the strength of your body, heart and lungs as well as easing the tension in your mind and spirit.

Benefits of jogging include:

- ☑ Enhanced lung capacity/Cardio health
- ☑ Weight loss/Calorie burn
- ☑ Strengthens muscles
- ☑ Builds stronger bones
- ☑ Relieves stress
- ☑ Stimulates endorphins
- ☑ Increases happiness
- ☑ Increases feelings of well being
- ☑ Improves sleep

Most importantly, you don't have to start off by running every day or long distances each time you jog. Just start by incorporating one minute of jogging while walking. A good trick I learned was to WALK FOUR MINUTES then JOG ONE MINUTE. Then repeat that pattern for half an hour.

Eventually, maybe after a month, you can reverse that pattern and WALK ONE MINUTE and JOG FOUR MINUTES.

This is a very easy way to add a small amount of jogging into your daily routine, and it works well. After only a few months, you'll be amazed how far you can actually jog without stopping. But pace yourself and go slowly until you feel ready to increase your time and distance. If you push too hard, you might injure yourself or get discouraged because you feel so out of breath. Take it easy and add a little time and distance each day so you don't burn yourself out. And always stay hydrated before and after your jog.

....

Health Tip: *Like hiking, jogging in nature is highly recommended. If you live anywhere near a park or lake, or if there's an easy dirt path through the woods or a meadow close to home, take advantage of this opportunity to enjoy the peace, quiet and fresh air of the great outdoors.*

BUILDING YOUR HOUSE (WEIGHTS)

Our muscular structure is the foundation of a healthy body, similar to the foundational structure of a well-built home. Ultimately, we want to build up our muscles as best we can. Not only will it make us feel better, stronger muscles will also help stabilize our posture, increase our endurance, slow the aging process, lower body fat, and make us look better. Increasing muscle mass is the ultimate goal for anyone who wants to improve their health, and it doesn't have to be a difficult task to accomplish.

I didn't start seriously working out with weights until I was around nine months sober. By that time I was walking, hiking and jogging on a daily basis. I was getting into good shape and had lost a significant amount of weight. My stomach pains had disappeared, my skin and hair were back to normal, I was sleeping soundly most nights, and my overall outlook on life was significantly improved. Combined with my 12-Step program, my life had improved beyond belief.

But I wanted to take it to the next level and found that weight lifting was the healthy, natural drug I had been missing out on my whole life.

I had had some experience with weight training when I was younger, during and after my college years. But I had slowly, over time, drifted away from it in pursuit of more decadent and destructive life choices. By the time I got back into it, I felt like a complete beginner again, so I needed to re-learn how to get started. Like with everything else we've been discussing, I needed to start slowly and *build myself up over time in small increments*. I joined a local gym and started weight training by using very light free weights and machines.

The most important thing to work on is your form. Form is everything when it comes to weight lifting. Without proper form, you are guaranteed to injure yourself, especially your back, shoulders and neck. So it's crucial to learn good form before anything else, especially before increasing the amount of weight you lift. So start with light weights and focus on form over anything else.

If you join a gym, most will offer a free one hour training session to get you started. If you can afford to hire a trainer, even for just a few sessions, I highly recommend it. If you're going to work out a home, ask a friend who is familiar with weight lifting to give you some pointers or to join you during your first few workouts. At the very least, watch some videos on weight lifting basics and safety. Do whatever it takes to learn good, safe form before you dive too deep into weight training.

The thing that I like best about lifting weights is how it makes me feel, right then and there. The endorphin rush can be euphoric. And your muscles love the attention they are receiving when they're being pumped with blood and oxygen each time you lift. Essential benefits of weight lifting:

- ☑ Improves overall strength and fitness
- ☑ Improves cardiovascular health
- ☑ Burns calories at a high rate
- ☑ Increases muscle mass
- ☑ Improves posture and balance
- ☑ Builds bone density
- ☑ Boosts energy
- ☑ Improves mood
- ☑ Reduces stress

Establishing a toned and healthy body is crucial to living a productive and successful life in sobriety. There are many ways you can achieve good health through exercise, as we've reviewed in the previous pages. Walking, stretching, dancing, yoga, hiking, jogging, swimming and weight lifting are just a few ways that you can reach your health goals. There many others you can try, and I encourage you to explore and experiment until you find what you enjoy and what best fits your life.

The most important point to take away from these suggestions is to get moving and to push your body to excel and improve. Exercise doesn't have to be a miserable, agonizing torture session. Most of the time, exercise in any form is gratifying, fun and can be moderately easy (but don't make it too easy or it won't work). Most importantly, you'll begin to feel better and better as long as you stick with it and keep trying to improve.

So get out there and move and groove, and never give up or get discouraged. You're building your body, like building a home, which takes time, care and focus. You deserve and need a healthy body. So start your health routine as soon as possible, and enjoy the journey to a better life.

....

*Health Tip: Your health routine should include three key elements—healthy food, consistent exercise and plenty of water. If you can create a daily routine consisting of these three basic elements, you will be on your way to significant physical improvement.

PART FOUR

SPIRITUAL HEALTH, SPIRITUAL WEALTH

*"We are not human beings having
a spiritual experience.
We are spiritual beings having a human experience."*
~ Pierre Teilhard de Chardin

SPIRITS IN THE MATERIAL WORLD

I n order to experience true, long lasting health, we need to acknowledge the importance of our spiritual and mental health. Many of the ideas we will discuss in the remaining chapters of this book have been covered in my book, <u>The Sober Journey: A Guide to Prayer and Meditation in Recovery</u>. However, I think they're important to include here also, in general terms, because our spiritual and mental health are intrinsic to our overall health. If you wish to explore the spiritual aspects of your recovery, I encourage you to take a peek at my other book which covers this subject in much more detail.

For now, we need to begin with the premise that we possess a spirit or soul. Yes, we are physical beings with bodies that grow, change and eventually deteriorate and die. We feel pain when we stub our toe. We feel nauseous and tired when we're sick. Our hair turns grey as we age. We enjoy the taste of food and the pleasures of sex. All these things are undeniably true. But there's much more to our experience on earth than our physical bodies.

It's important to accept (or at the very least *consider*) the idea that there is more to you than just a body made of skin and bones. Your personality, your essence, that indefinable thing called *you* is much more than just a bunch of molecules and atoms slamming together in a cold, random universe. You are life itself, ever expanding, striving, thriving, forever moving forward and upward through infinite changes and possibilities.

You are a *spiritual being*, having a physical experience. This may sound strange at first, like you're an alien (spirit) visiting a planet (your body). But in a way this is true. Our bodies are like vehicles that transport our personalities from one location to another while we're on earth. Our bodies are a part of our life experience, and should be respected and enjoyed for the pleasures they bring. But the essence of who we are as individuals comes from something else; not from our fingers and toes, but from our ideas, thoughts and feelings.

There is a spirit within you that is beyond the physical. There is a soul within you that craves something more than just food, sex and other physical pleasures. There is a desire deep within the human soul for understanding and enlightenment, wisdom and love. These things, love in particular, come from a place that cannot be seen, heard or touched. They can only be felt from the inner core of your being. They can only be discovered and experienced through a spiritual journey.

I believe that religion, and any spiritual path is an individual choice that should be respected by everyone. How you choose to understand and draw closer to your Higher Power is entirely up to you. All the major religions grapple with the same basic questions and all have developed some degree of truth about human spirituality. But it's important to keep your mind open and available to new ideas and possibilities. You can't learn anything new if you shut down your mind. The most important thing when starting on a new journey—especially a spiritual journey—is to keep an open mind and heart. Test new ideas. Consider new information. Find what resonates for you personally and disregard what doesn't work.

It's important to remember that no one has a monopoly on the truth when it comes to religion and spirituality. Yes, there are religious leaders and cultists who will claim they have a direct line to God and only they know the truth. But usually people who make such claims have something to sell or are seeking power and fame.

One of the great elements of Buddhism is an emphasis on belief in the teaching, not the teacher. No matter how charismatic, entertaining, attractive or wise a teacher might be, it's crucial not to become trapped in a cult of personality where the person teaching becomes more important than the teaching itself.

History is filled with the tragic consequences of people following a mesmerizing personality to the gates of hell. Learn from others wherever you can. But recognize when a teacher is offering wisdom and love instead of demanding conformity and blind loyalty.

The most important teacher you will ever find is *you*. Learn to trust your own inner voice. Follow your own spiritual quest instead of adhering to what someone else is telling you. Yes, there are many things you can learn from other people, and I hope I can offer a few kernels of wisdom that will help you move forward in your journey. Recognizing that you have an inner voice that will teach and guide you more than you can imagine.

There is a spirit within you connected to something beyond your physical being. Part of your sober journey is accepting that you have a spiritual aspect to your life that needs to be explored, respected, and cherished. Don't be afraid to learn all that you can about your spirit and, if you're willing, you will discover faith in a Higher Power that will nurture your soul.

TRY TO HAVE A
LITTLE FAITH

For many years I relied only on my own ego to survive. I tried to do everything on my own, blindly putting all my faith in my own ability to control the world and the universe. I thought I was in charge and that no one could do a better job at running my life than me, no matter how much pain and self-destruction I created along the way. Not surprisingly, I ended up a broke, sick and miserable alcoholic. What a shocker!

The moment I gave up trying to run the universe and handed my life over to a power greater than myself, everything changed. I took myself out of the driver's seat and became a passenger on the road of life. Sounds corny, perhaps, but it works.

I didn't worry about what to call my Higher Power. I didn't have to assign a name to it. I joyfully gave up fighting and gave in to a faith in something beyond me, finally recognizing that the Source of all life was *for* me, not *against* me. Once I was able to accept this idea, I found I was much more relaxed in my daily affairs. I no longer felt I needed to force life to work the way I demanded it to work. Instead, I was able to release my life and my will over to something bigger than me. I immediately felt lighter, experienced less depression and fear, and began to enjoy my life more and more each day. I began to feel joy again and there is no better spiritual medicine than a good shot of joy to fuel your body, mind and spirit.

. . . .

Quick Tip: *Memorize and repeat daily the most important prayer in recovery: The Serenity Prayer. It works.*

THE POWER OF PRAYER

Prayer is a word everyone has heard, like air or love. But what *is* prayer and how can it help you improve your life and health?

An important part of prayer is a willingness to trust that there is something beyond what we can see and a reliance on what can only be felt through intuition. Prayer is simply a way for us, using our minds, to communicate with God, or Spirit, just like turning on a lamp is a way for us to receive light. As we discussed earlier, you are a spiritual being having a physical experience here on earth. But God is pure spirit. So, in order to communicate with God, we need to use our minds—the one part of ourselves that is most closely aligned with our spiritual nature.

Prayer is the act of direct communication, using our minds, in an effort to activate a relationship with God or Spirit. Prayer is nothing more than a pathway, or channel, that directs our thoughts, fears, desires and hopes towards a Higher Power. Prayer often brings us a sense of calm and an easing of anxiety and depression, which ultimately enhances our journey that we're on to improve our health.

Prayer doesn't have to be complicated nor esoteric. In order to pray we simply need to speak clearly with our Higher Power as we understand it, asking for clarity, strength and inspiration. Daily prayer is one of the best gifts you can give yourself and will enhance your life significantly if you're open, honest and humble.

....

*Quick Tip:** *Pick a time each day, perhaps in the morning or just before bed, to kneel and simply say "Thank You." Sometimes that alone is enough to nourish your soul and fill your heart with gratitude.*

BENEFITS OF MEDITATION

Meditation is an amazing and proven way to improve your spiritual and mental health and can be practiced by anyone, just about anywhere, any time.

There are countless ways to describe meditation and countless books on the subject. I encourage you to read and investigate everything available on the topic. But for our purposes, I think the easiest way to describe meditation is to simply call it *mind training*.

If we can go to the gym to train our bodies, then we can go to our minds to train our thinking. Every time we practice meditation, we're trying to train our minds to be calm and quiet and to accept life as it is. In 12-Step circles, this is known as *life on life's terms*.

When I first tried to meditate, the noise in my brain was so loud and confusing I actually thought I might be insane. That's not an exaggeration. I seriously thought there was something wrong with me and that I might be losing touch with reality.

Every time I closed my eyes to meditate, I was confronted by multiple thoughts and ideas, all crashing together, each one demanding my attention. There was a tornado of activity swirling inside my head. But I was unable to hold a single thought for more than a few seconds before another idea or disturbing image would blow through the door of my subconscious and twist and spin across my brain.

I would quickly open my eyes, startled by the chaos inside my mind. Some thoughts were simple and amusing while others were strange and frightening. Then I would close my eyes and try again, only to quickly open them as soon as the thought-storm commenced. It was overwhelming.

Who the hell wants to do this? I asked myself. *This sucks!*

Thankfully, I stuck with it and never gave up. I hope you do the same. Over several weeks and months, I slowly began to incorporate simple techniques that allowed me to sit for longer and longer periods of time with my eyes closed while I tried my best to focus on my breath. Being able to sit with my eyes closed for five minutes was a huge accomplishment. Eventually I could sit for twenty to thirty minutes peacefully. But it took time and patience.

When I began meditation, I was searching for a way to find serenity. I knew I had a disturbed and restless ("untrained") mind. If there was a way for me to quiet the noise in my head and soothe my aching spirit, I was determined to find it. Meditation was, and is, one of the most important factors in my daily life. It has helped me immensely by calming the storms that once raged inside my head. There are many ways to practice meditation. Like prayer, you have to find what works best for you. Most importantly, you should experiment and enjoy the journey. Meditation will help you discover how your mind operates and how to calm it. You don't have to be a hippie or a Buddhist monk either. Meditation is there for anyone and everyone who can find a few minutes in their day to pause and look inward. It is one of the most effective ways I have discovered to improve my mental and spiritual health and happiness.

....

Quick Tip: *There are numerous ways to learn how to meditate including books (***The Sober Journey: A Guide to Prayer and Meditation in Recovery** *written by yours truly is a good place to start), videos and local classes in your town or city.*

THE SPIRITUAL FRUIT OF LOVE

There is no greater force in the universe than love. Without love, a mother would not feed her child. Without love, mankind would never have evolved beyond the grunting stage of cave dwellers. There would be no kindness or compassion in the world. Without love, we would have no reason to exist. Love is the nourishment that feeds our soul and illuminates our being.

Love gives life meaning. And love is not exclusive to humans—it is the universal, spiritual essence permeating *all* life on earth. All creatures on earth seem to have some capacity to give and receive love. Just ask anyone who owns a dog or cat. Or, consider how primates care for one another.

Where does love come from? What is it, exactly? Nobody has ever *seen* love. We only see the *effects* of love. Love is something that can be felt—not something you can hold in your hand like a coin. And yet we can certainly agree that love is real.

Both the gardener and the farmer know that they can't plant an apple seed and expect to grow a watermelon. This would defy the laws of nature as we know them. *We reap exactly what we sow.* And so it is with love. When we plant seeds of love in our lives, we reap the spiritual rewards of what we have sown—*friendship, harmony, peace, joy and gratitude.* Love begets love, just as anger begets anger and hate begets hate.

For so long, I lived on a steady diet of anger and resentment while I was still trapped in my addiction. Even going to the local coffee shop tested my state of mind. A wrong look from someone or a perceived insult (usually imagined) would fill me with contempt for human beings. It got so bad that I started to believe that people actually didn't like me, regardless of whether they knew me or not. I became paranoid and distrustful of everyone. It saddens me to think back on how much time I wasted worrying about what others felt and thought about me, mostly because none of it was true.

As I began my own sober journey, I learned that in order to receive love, I first need to learn how to love myself and how to give love. It's not complicated, nor is it a revolutionary new idea. Mankind learned long ago that the power of love is what keeps us alive, fulfilled and happy. Without it, humans would've disappeared from earth long ago. Without love, society would collapse.

Everyone needs, wants and deserves love. There is no creature on earth that doesn't benefit from or want love. So it is imperative that you plant seeds of love in your mind often, every day; spiritual seeds that that will grow in your daily life and bear the fruit of joy, serenity and peace,

....

*Quick Tip: *In your daily prayers, get in the habit of asking how you can be more forgiving and loving to others, even towards people you don't like. Begin looking at your own anger and resentments during prayer and ask how you can change them to love for other human beings.

DO UNTO OTHERS

There have been many times in my life when I spent so much time obsessing over how I was *feeling* that I forgot to focus on things I could actually be *doing*. "Navel gazing" is defined as self-indulgent or excessive contemplation of oneself or a single issue, at the expense of a wider view. This is a concept I know all too well. I'm guilty of spending far too much time over-thinking and obsessing about things that really aren't that important, usually things about myself that no one in their right mind would really care about.

Too often we become trapped in a never-ending cycle of inner reflection and self-analysis. This can easily devolve into self-obsession and selfishness. Another way to put it is "analysis paralysis," the phenomenon of spending so much time analyzing our own situation, that we become spiritually paralyzed and useless to others who might need our help. It's very easy to allow ourselves to wallow in self-reflection, whether we're thinking about how sad we are (*"woe-is-me-ism"*) or how great we are (*"damn-I'm-awesome-ism"*).

Not that inner reflection is always a bad thing. In fact, it can be an important part of healing and recovery from many things, including addiction or heartbreak. But we need to be careful not to get stuck in our inner-world. Otherwise, we face the danger of becoming isolated and separated from the outer-world.

We should always do our best to look outward, beyond our own self, to the world around us. The easiest way to do this is to seek opportunities to make ourselves available to serve others. Service gets us out of our own heads and focuses our attention away from ourselves.

If you can simply start each day with the question, "How can I be of service to others today?" you'll be amazed by the number of service opportunities that appear in your daily life. Just putting the question out there is enough to spark an acute awareness of those around you who might be in distress.

Your job isn't to save the world. Instead, it's just a matter of showing a small kindness—perhaps talking to someone who feels sad or lonely, offering a genuine compliment, or giving a ride to someone who doesn't own a car. There are countless ways we can be of service to others every day, and by simply stating it in prayer, the opportunities will present themselves.

....

*Quick Tip: Set a goal to do one kind thing for someone today. It doesn't have to be anything big or fancy. Just give someone, even a stranger, a genuine compliment or ask them if they're doing okay. You'll be amazed how many people respond positively to your gesture of kindness.

SPIRITUAL PATHS

There countless ways to pursue a healthy, spiritual path in your life. I have mentioned only a few. What's important is that you try to develop a life filled with spiritual pursuits, curiosity and practice. Otherwise, what's the point of everything? Are we here on earth just to live like any other animal -- eating, pooping, sleeping and screwing? Is that it?

That pretty much describes the life of your average goat or chicken. I don't know about you, but I'm searching for more than the life of a chicken while I'm here on earth! I want to LIVE! I want to FEEL! I want to EXPERIENCE! I want to LOVE! I want to LEARN! I want to LAUGH and CRY! I want to hear MUSIC! I want seek GOD or whatever put it all together! I want to explore ART! I want to feel PASSION! I want to live a life filled with all the wonderful gifts that have been given to us beyond just the physical parts of our existence.

Don't sit around waiting for spiritual enlightenment. It usually won't arrive on its own. To find it, you have to seek it. Start by exploring books on spirituality and religion. Go to church, synagogue or temple if you want to search for God with others. Begin praying and meditating. Learn about Buddhism. Attend a yoga class or a meditation retreat. Spend more time in nature. Listen to spiritual music. Attend a 12-Step meeting to absorb and enjoy the spiritual power of fellowship with other recovering addicts.

There are so many spiritual paths to explore. Don't ever be afraid to try new things, especially spiritual pursuits. Activate your heart and mind and explore the infinite wonders of life seen and unseen.

PART FIVE

THE POWER OF POSITIVITY

"Change your thoughts and you
can change your world."
~ Noman Vincent Peale

HEALTHY MIND, HEALTHY BODY

Do you see the glass half empty or half full? According to the Mayo Clinic, positive thinking helps with stress management, can improve your health, and increase your life span. The simple and obvious fact is that if you cultivate a positive attitude in life, you might live longer, will be more joyful, and will experience less anxiety, stress and fear.

Positivity has been proven to benefit you in many ways including:

- ☑ Lowers distress
- ☑ Reduces fear
- ☑ Reduces anxiety
- ☑ Reduces depression
- ☑ Improves cardiovascular health
- ☑ Improves overall physical health
- ☑ Increases life span
- ☑ Improves our interaction with other people
- ☑ Improves friendships and family relationships

☑ Helps with addiction recovery

You don't have to be a genius to realize that positive, upbeat people are more pleasant and enjoyable to be around, and generally have more friends than your average angry drunk. One of the many challenges that recovering alcoholics and addicts face is their inability or, more often, unwillingness to let go of resentment and anger for the perceived injustices they have suffered. *Woe-is-me-ism* is a real and far too common mental ailment that plagues many addicts in the early stages of recovery. The idea that we've been dealt a bad hand in life too often follows people into early sobriety and often results in relapse. Don't let this happen to you!

Here's the bottom line: You have to knock that shit off! Negativity gets you nowhere fast. Negativity and pessimism are part of the reason so many of us end up broken and defeated from our addictions in the first place. So why carry it into our sobriety and possibly destroy our effort to recover?

Resentment, the worst form of negativity, is one of the most lethal and toxic poisons we can swallow (we'll discuss resentment in the next section). And we've been ingesting a lot of poison over the years, so there's no reason to continue.

It's important to develop a positive attitude and outlook on life. There are a few simple things we can do to brighten up our day and, more importantly, improve someone else's day. The first thing we need to do is recognize when we're being sullen, angry, spiteful or vengeful in any way. All of these negative emotions are easy to detect because they feel bad, much like a hangover. When you're feeling less-than-positive, check yourself and try to adjust your attitude toward a more positive way of thinking.

Like our spiritual health, our mental health has a huge impact on our life in recovery. So it's crucial that you begin to notice any negativity you're carrying around and learn how to replace it with the power of positivity.

GRATITUDE

Of all the things we should focus on if we want to enjoy a positive outlook on life, gratitude is unquestionably the most important place to start. It would be easy to argue that love is the most important thing, and to a certain extent I agree. But until we are truly grateful for who we are and what we have, our ability to give and receive love is significantly blocked by festering resentment. How can we possibly find happiness and peace, and give and receive true love, until we first acknowledge and express gratitude for the blessings we already possess?

When I first got sober, I was filled with resentment and rage. I felt that I had been cheated out of having the life I thought I "deserved". I *deserved* a better life! I *deserved* more money, better friends, a perfect body, a trophy wife, a large house, fame and fortune.

How could I possibly be responsible for the crappy condition of my life and the way it turned out? The world, and everyone in it, was to blame—not me! It was never my fault; it was all someone else's fault. Didn't the world recognize my awesomeness?

I was blinded by resentment and unable to see the part I played in my own self-destruction. I felt entitled to something better than what I had.

So, the question is this: how do we begin to focus on gratitude when we don't feel any gratitude and don't know where to find it?

It's very simple. Start with where you are right now!

Look around you. I guarantee that you will find something that you can appreciate. It can be anything. Perhaps it's the fact that you have two hands and two feet that work (assuming you do); or maybe you have a roof over your head; or maybe you have something delicious in your kitchen that you can eat later; or there's a good television show on tonight that you enjoy.

If you try hard enough, you will always be able to find at least one or two things to be grateful for—a favorite pet; a good meal; a soft pillow to sleep on; a song you love; a funny joke; a good cup of coffee. Or maybe you can find gratitude in being able to help another person who is also struggling or suffering (another recovering addict, for instance).

Start with the simple things in your life. Don't focus on the negatives, only on a few things that make you smile or bring you comfort. Find the small things in life that you're grateful for and expand your outlook from there over time.

....

*Quick Tip: *Start keeping a gratitude journal. Each morning or evening, write down three thigs that you are grateful for, any person, place or thing that brings you joy.*

STOP RESISTING

Learning to live in acceptance is the key to a positive mind. When we use the term "acceptance," we're not talking about resignation, which implies giving up or allowing bad things to happen. We're not doormats to be stepped on. Acceptance for us means *non-resistance*. We want to be able to reach a point where we can *accept* things that happen in our life (and in our mind) and observe them without fear or judgment. We need to learn how to "*Roll with it, baby!*"

To use a well-worn sports analogy, life throws us a lot of curve balls. It often seems that our problems appear out of nowhere. We start the day with a certain set of expectations, only to be thrown a curve ball that catches us off guard, sometimes hitting us square in the face.

When we become too fixated and attached to how things *should be* instead of accepting how of things *actually are*, we become trapped in an endless cycle of disappointment and frustration.

Some days we're hit by more than one curve ball at a time. Then we find ourselves trying to fix one problem while confronting another. We become overwhelmed and can easily succumb to frustration and anger. At this point, we might want to just throw our hands up in the air and resign ourselves to our miserable fate.

But there's another path we can take: *acceptance.*

One of the greatest phrases I always keep in mind is *"This too shall pass."*

The fact is *all* things shall pass eventually. Nothing is permanent. Bad, unpleasant or frightening things all end at some point. The same is true for good things. *All things shall pass.* The trick is to accept conditions as impermanent rather than obsessing over or attaching ourselves to anything, either good or bad.

One moment might seem perfect; the next moment might be filled with problems. One day you might be dating your soul mate; the next day your heart is broken. One week you might feel healthy; the next week you're sick. One month you might have extra money in the bank; the next month you're flat broke.

All of these are passing conditions. Nothing is permanent and nothing stays the same. The only thing we can rely on is change itself. Change is the only constant. Both the bad and the good will all pass into something else at some point. If we can accept this fact, if we can live in *acceptance of what is, rather than what should be,* we will find it much easier to live in harmony with the fluctuations and changes that confront us every day.

Again, we don't want to be doormats and let life (or people) trample over us. We have to take responsibility and fix things that need to be fixed. But it's also important to realize that life is filled with ups and downs and there is no such thing as perfection.

Sometimes you'll be overwhelmed by negative thoughts or difficult situations, all demanding your attention at the same time. Instead of fighting and resisting, just accept without judgment or fear. When you're being bombarded by problems, simply remind yourself of this truth: "*This too shall pass.*" Then smile and get to work fixing whatever needs to be fixed.

REMIND YOURSELF DAILY

t's important that we empty our minds of negative thoughts each day, replacing those dark ideas with positive, uplifting reminders of how interesting, amusing and wondrous life can be. The point is to feed our souls with nourishing words that provide uplifting and transcendent thoughts and ideas.

If you were to take a glass filled with dirty, brown pond water and hold it under a dripping faucet, eventually the drops of water from the sink would replace the dirty pond water. The glass would then be filled with water clean enough to drink and nourish your body. This is similar to how positive thought works. We add a steady drip of daily positive wisdom into our minds that feeds and nourishes our souls.

There are many ways that you can feed your soul and nourish your mind, including a passage from the Bible, a Buddhist chant or a beautiful poem or song. But it's important that you become aware of what you're feeding your mind each day. What you feed your mind and soul is just as important as what you feed your body. Fill your body with junk food, you'll get physically sick. Fill your mind with negativity, you'll become mentally sick.

Are you drinking a glass filled with dirty pond water or clean, spring water? Are you living on a steady diet of negativity and pessimism or positivity and hope? Remind yourself every day, all day long if you have to, that life is good, that you're a good person, that most people are trying to be good, and that all your struggles and efforts are worth it. Develop a healthy habit of positive thoughts and ideas that will sustain you today and bring you hope for tomorrow.

NEGATIVE MEDIA

As we near the end of this book, I want to spend a moment discussing the negative forces behind social media, the daily news and the violence permeating television and movies.

We live in a time in history when we're bombarded, every hour of every day, by a barrage of negativity, anger, resentment, envy and division. Just turn on the television and you'll witness a parade of newscasters and pundits screaming about politics and trying their best to divide the country further. Go on social media and you'll be flooded with anger and resentment by a million anonymous trolls all demanding one thing or another from society (*resentment* seems to be a form of currency on social media).

Everywhere we look at media these days there's an overwhelming amount of anger, hate and negativity being spewed forth by fools, pundits and clowns.

The best thing we can do, the wisest path we can follow, is to avoid or ignore all this social and media poison as much as we can. It's almost impossible to avoid it completely, but we don't have to live in it by the hour either. Do your best to absorb as little social and news media as possible. Instead of watching the news on TV, watch The Disney Channel or your favorite comedy. Instead of looking at Facebook for hours, read a book or take a walk. Rather than looking at all the fools on Instagram showing off their supposedly perfect lives, have lunch with a friend, go fishing or hit the gym.

We spend so much time these days drowning in negative media. And it's hurting us all, in my opinion. So do yourself a favor and shut off the news pundits and the social media haters. Enjoy your life away from the screens and the screaming. Life is pretty damn good, no matter what all the idiots in the negative media are trying to tell you every second.

BRINGING IT ALL HOME

Assuming you've made it this far in this book, chances are good that you're sober and working on your recovery. Most likely, you'll recognize that your physical, mental and spiritual health has been compromised by years of addiction. Hopefully you've begun implementing, or experimenting with, some of the suggestions I've presented. My greatest hope and desire is that you've started to work on your health journey and that you're reaping the rewards of building a stronger body and more positive outlook on life.

If you're anything like me, you've spent years struggling in addiction. Now you're on a sober journey that will lead you to a better, more productive and successful life. Let's be honest; we didn't get sober to be less productive and successful, so we need to do everything we can within out power to improve ourselves. Getting and staying sober means more than not drinking and using. Long-term sobriety depends upon daily effort at staying clean, avoiding bad decisions, rebuilding our lives, and improving our health.

If you're reading this book, you're probably on the right path, and I wish you well. Your sobriety should include working with other recovering addicts, attending 12-Step meetings (if that's part of your recovery), helping others get sober and creating the foundation for a new life in recovery. Your physical and mental health is extremely important to your recovery and should never be ignored or set aside. Pay attention to your nutrition, exercise frequently, develop a spiritual life and stay positive.

Your life in sobriety is the most important journey you will ever travel. Take good care of your body, mind and spirit, and you will reap the infinite rewards.

May your life be happy, joyous and free.

PART SIX

ROUTINES & RECIPES

The following is a simple plan you can follow to get started on your exercise routine. This is just a suggestion and is not meant to be a definitive workout, but only a way to get you started. It's a very easy program to follow that will bring you results, help you feel better and give you more energy. You can either try this plan, or use it as an outline to create your own plan. Just do what works best for you and enjoy the journey.

Easy 12 Week Exercise Plan

Week 1-- (6 Days Per Week)
- ☑ 10 Minute Walk 2X or 3X Per Day

Week 2 -- (6 Days Per Week)
- ☑ 5 Minutes of Stretching in the Morning
- ☑ 15 Minute Walk 2X Per Day

Week 3 -- (6 Days Per Week)
- ☑ 10 Minutes of Stretching in the Morning
- ☑ 20 Minute Walk 2X per Day

Week 4 -- (6 Days Per Week)
- ☑ 10 Minutes of stretching in the Morning

☑ 20 Minute Walk 2x Per Day
☑ 10 Minutes of Stretch in the Evening

Week 5 -- (6 Days Per Week)
☑ 10 Minutes of Stretching in the Morning
☑ 30 Minute Walk 1X Per Day
☑ 10 Minutes of Stretching in the Evening

Week 6 -- (5 Days Per Week)
☑ 15 Minutes of Stretching in the Morning
☑ 45 Minute Walk 1X Per Day
☑ 15 Minutes of Stretch in the Evening

Week 7 -- (5 Days Per Week)
☑ 15 Minutes of Stretching in the Morning
☑ 60 Minute Walk or Easy Uphill Hike 1X Per Day
☑ 15 Minutes of Stretch in the Evening

Week 8—(5 Days Per Week)
☑ 15 Minutes of Stretching in the Morning
☑ 60 Minute Walk or Easy Uphill Hike 1X Per Day
☑ 15 Minutes of Stretch in the Evening

Week 9—(5 Days Per Week)
☑ 15 Minutes of Stretching in the Morning
☑ Walk 4 Minutes/Jog 1 Minute (Continue for 30 Minutes)
☑ 15 Minutes of Stretch in the Evening

Week 10—(5 Days Per Week)
- ☑ 15 Minutes of Stretching in the Morning
- ☑ Walk 4 Minutes/Jog 1 Minute (Continue for 30 Minutes)
- ☑ 15 Minutes of Stretch in the Evening

Week 11—(5 Days Per Week)
- ☑ 15 Minutes of Stretching in the Morning
- ☑ Walk 1 Minutes/Jog 4 Minutes (Continue for 30 Minutes)
- ☑ 15 Minutes of Stretch in the Evening

Week 12—(5 Days Per Week)
- ☑ 15 Minutes of Stretching in the Morning
- ☑ Jog 15 Minutes/Walk 15 Minutes
- ☑ 15 Minutes of Stretch in the Evening

1. After 12 weeks you can start lifting light weights, either at home or a local gym.
2. Add yoga, hiking, dancing, jogging, swimming or any cardio activity that you enjoy.
3. Eat healthy every day and drink at least eight 8-ounce glasses of water daily.

SMOOTHIE RECIPES

'm a big believer in smoothies. I think they're the easiest way to make a meal that is healthy and tastes great. I prefer to have at least one per day, usually in the morning. They can be used as meal replacements, an afternoon snack or simply as a way to supercharge your intake of natural vitamins, fiber and nutrients. Below are a few of my favorite smoothie recipes. But you can add anything you want as you experiment with your own smoothie creations.

Banana Apple Smoothie

- ☑ 1 Banana
- ☑ 1 Apple or Pear
- ☑ 1 Large Handful Raw Spinach
- ☑ 1 Cup Almond Milk (or any type of milk)
- ☑ 1 Large Scoop Vanilla Protein Powder
- ☑ 1 Cup of Ice
- ☑ Blend until Smooth

Apple Berry Smoothie
- ☑ 1 Apple (Red or Green)
- ☑ 1 Cup Blueberries (or any berries)
- ☑ 1 Large Handful Raw Spinach
- ☑ 1 Cup Almond Milk (or any type of milk)
- ☑ 1 Large Scoop Vanilla Protein Powder
- ☑ 1 Cup Ice
- ☑ Blend Until Smooth

Green Smoothie
- ☑ 1 Apple or Banana
- ☑ 1 Large Handful Raw Spinach
- ☑ 1 Large Handful Raw Kale Leaves (no stems)
- ☑ 1 Large Celery Stem
- ☑ 1 Cup Apple or Pineapple Juice
- ☑ 2 Scoops Vanilla Protein Powder
- ☑ 1 Cup Ice
- ☑ Blend Until Smooth

*If you enjoyed reading this book, will you please take a moment to leave an honest review on: **www. Amazon.com** or **www.barnesandnoble.com**

Thank you very much.

If you would like to join our community, please visit us at:
Website: www.thesoberjourney.com
Facebook: www.facebook.com/sobertravels/

Other Books by Dirk Foster:
<u>**The Sober Journey: A Guide to Prayer and Meditation in Recovery**</u>

Made in the USA
Middletown, DE
04 July 2020